Ralph Ellison and
the Politics of the Novel

Ralph Ellison and
the Politics of the Novel

H. William Rice

LEXINGTON BOOKS
Lanham • Boulder • New York • Oxford

LEXINGTON BOOKS

Published in the United States of America
by Lexington Books
An imprint of The Rowman & Littlefield Publishing Group, Inc.
4501 Forbes Boulevard, Suite 200, Lanham, Maryland 20706

PO Box 317
Oxford
OX2 9RU, UK

British Library Cataloguing in Publication Information Available

Library of Congress Cataloging-in-Publication Data

Rice, Herbert William, 1952–
    Ralph Ellison and the politics of the novel / H. William Rice.
        p. cm.
    Includes bibliographical references and index.
    ISBN 0-7391-0654-6 (cloth : alk. paper)
    1. Ellison, Ralph—Authorship. 2. Ellison, Ralph—Political and social views.
    3. Politics and literature—United States—History—20th century. 4. African
    Americans in literature. I. Title.

    PS3555.L625Z874 2003
    818'.5409—dc21   2003005112

Printed in the United States of America

For my parents—

The late Reverend Herbert W. Rice
and Nancy M. Rice

They lived and embodied that most radical of American ideals:
That all Men are created Equal.

Contents

Acknowledgments   ix

Introduction   1

1. The Invisible Man in Ralph Ellison's *Invisible Man*   7

2. The Magic and the Mystery of Words   25

3. A Socially Responsible Role for an Invisible Man:
    Ellison the Essayist   57

4. Outside History   91

5. *Juneteenth*: The Coon Cage Eight and the Joe Cah   113

Conclusion   133

Index   143

About the Author   151

Acknowledgments

This book began with ideas picked up from numerous sources. Though the foundation of this book was not a dissertation, some of the ideas with which it began grew out of various classes that I took in the Ph.D. program at The University of Georgia. Two classes in particular gave me ideas that I was to ruminate on for ten years: Professor Mike Moran's Literature and Rhetoric course in the Winter of 1990 and Professor Christy Desmet's Modern Issues in Rhetorical Theory course in the Spring of 1990. As these ideas began to germinate, there were various people whose conversations, teaching, and ideas were influential. The late Dr. Thelma Hall and her husband Dr. Wilson Hall of Shorter College were always part of my continuing conversation about American literature. Dr. Steve Sheeley, Professor of Religion and Assistant Vice-President for Academic Affairs at Shorter College, has also been an avid conversant of mine. He and I bounce ideas off each other on a daily basis. Dr. Carmen Butcher graciously offered to edit one of the final versions of the manuscript. Her close reading was instrumental in helping me get the manuscript into final shape. Finally, my childhood friend and old roommate Dr. Rodney Allen, author and English professor at the Louisiana School for Math, Science, and the Arts, is someone whose ideas and statements have always been important to every project in which I have been involved. Kim Herndon, Dean of Libraries at Shorter College, has checked on me during periods when this project has nearly driven me to madness. She has also been ready to help me whenever I needed to get research advice or even to borrow a blues recording. Dr. Harold Newman, the "Boss" at Shorter College, has been my running partner for over twenty years and has created the kind of school and faculty in which I am proud to work. Without his friendship and support none of my work would have been possible. Finally, the Professional Development Committee at Shorter under the leadership of Dr. Jan Jones and later Mr. Stephen Frazier provided me with two grants which helped to finance my research at the Library of Congress.

Then there were the more personal contributions. Ansley, my wife, and Will and Matthew, my children, have put up with me for all of these years. (And sometimes it has not been easy.) They make my life a happy one. Along with my wife and children, my brother Dan has always been my closest confidant in all matters of the heart and soul. I owe him more than I can ever repay. And finally, there were the contributions of my parents, the late Reverend Herbert William Rice and Nancy Mason Rice. They raised me and my brothers, Dan and John, in a racially divided South. Somehow in the process they taught us to value all people of all colors, even those white southerners that made our lives and those of other civil rights sympathizers and advocates miserable.

I should also like to thank the staff of the Manuscripts Division at the Library of Congress in Washington, D. C. Alice Birney, a member of that team, was particularly helpful in expediting my research. I also thank the staff at Lexington Books for helping me get this book into publishable form. Jason Hallman and Brian Richards were both thoughtful and precise in their guidance. I thank Mrs. Fanny Ellison and Dr. John Callahan for giving me permission to quote from Ralph Ellison's published work as well as his unpublished manuscripts at the Library of Congress. I also thank Dr. Callahan for his tireless work to make the rest of Ellison's writing available to us. Without his persistence, his labor, and his critical insights, the picture we have of Ralph Ellison would be considerably diminished. Professor Callahan was also extremely generous to me with his time, reading my manuscript and giving me advice on the portions that cover *Juneteenth*. He was also willing to talk with me about his impressions of Ellison. Ralph Ellison could not have left his work in the hands of a finer executor than John Callahan. Other critics were instrumental in bringing Ellison to life for me through their work. Among them were Houston Baker, Robert O'Meally, Horace Porter, Jerry Watts, and Lawrence Jackson. Finally, I should like to thank the late Ralph Ellison for writing books that changed us all and for struggling heroically with the most American of forms—the novel.

Introduction

*"One fact I am sure about: the writing of novels is the damnedest thing that I
ever got into, and I've been into some damnable things."*
—Ralph Ellison, "The Novel as a Function of American Democracy"

Ralph Waldo Ellison's reputation rests primarily on one novel published in 1952 when he was thirty-eighty years old. He wrote, published, and lectured extensively until he died at eighty, but during that time he did not publish another novel. Furthermore, nothing that he published in those forty-two years came close to the stature of that one book. All of his publications after *Invisible Man* gained some measure of credence from the fact that they were the work of the author of that one amazing 1952 novel. Though there are certainly great American writers who have produced only one book—Jean Toomer and Harper Lee come to mind—there are none who have established and maintained a reputation as a major writer based on only one book. In that regard Ellison is unique. As Terrence Rafferty stated using a baseball analogy that works well in the setting of American literature, Ellison pitched a perfect game on his first time on the mound.[1] But perhaps more curious even than that astounding no-hitter is the fact that Ellison stayed in the bullpen for the next forty-two years without ever pitching again.

Though such a summation of Ellison's career runs the risk of minimizing his considerable contributions to the essay, literary criticism, the short story, jazz, and American culture in general, it does underscore a central critical problem that those who would write about Ellison must always face. What does one do with the question of the second novel? If Ellison had abandoned literature for other endeavors after *Invisible Man,* much as French poet Arthur Rimbaud supposedly abandoned poetry for big game hunting, the critic could simply argue that the writer's interests changed. He was a writer and then he was not. But Ellison's pursuit of his second novel was dogged. By the time he had reached old age, his problems in completing the second novel were almost as legendary as *Invisible Man* itself. Even external events that played a role in the delay in finishing the novel were legendary, as John Callahan has commented.[2] The 1967 fire that burned Ellison's Plainfield home in the Berkshires, and with it the only existing copy of important portions of the manuscript, was forever the blow of fate that played its role in the delay in finishing the novel. To his credit, Ellison never entirely blamed the fire. He also blamed himself, writing as early as 1963 in "The World and the Jug," his famous reply to Irving Howe's "Black Boys and Native Sons," that to his reader's demand that he publish more novels, he was "remiss and vulnerable, perhaps."[3] Still, thirty years later, he was only more remiss and more vulnerable because the novel had yet to appear.

The question of the second novel was in part resolved and in part further complicated by the posthumous publication in 1999 (five years after Ellison's death) of *Juneteenth*, a portion of the manuscript of the second novel. John Callahan, Ellison's literary executor, did a careful job of selecting the published segment from the mammoth manuscript that Ellison left. But even if that work in some ways allows the critic a glimpse at what Ellison was doing for those forty-two years, it creates more questions. What compelled him not to publish this novel, since he apparently had something ready to set forth as early as 1959? Further, what else did he leave? The second question will be answered when Callahan publishes the scholarly edition of the Ellison manuscript and opens all of the Ellison manuscripts at the Library of Congress for scholarly review. But the first question will never be fully answered and deepens the mystery that surrounds Ellison's work.

The ebb and flow of Ellison's status as an American writer also complicates the matter. His failure to write another novel, plus his consistent refusal to be an active participant in any demonstrations or protests during the Civil Rights movement made many of his colleagues question his political allegiance to black causes. This problem was exacerbated immeasurably by other political positions with which he aligned himself. He persisted in using the word "negro" long after that word had become offensive to most African Americans.[4] Furthermore, he spoke on behalf of the Johnson administration during some of the darkest days of the Vietnam conflict. These sorts of activities led to the familiar charge that Ellison was the proverbial Uncle Tom, currying favor with the white literati at the expense of his own integrity as both a writer and an African American.

Though few careful readers of Ellison would take this charge seriously, Ellison does stand before us as a great, unfinished work of art, as tantalizing somehow in what it promises as in the amazing wealth it provides. And though Ellison himself shied away from direct political involvement during his literary life, the time during which he wrote as well as the content of what he wrote forever pushes forward the question of politics. The novel itself is a very political form, growing as it did out of eighteenth-century British culture, a culture that by the time the novel came along had beheaded one king and severely restricted the divine rights of those who followed him to the throne. As it developed, it became the genre of the middle class, reflecting the concerns and frustrations of everyday life. Ellison was keenly aware of this fact, writing in "The Novel as a Function of American Democracy" in 1967, "As I see it, the novel has always been bound up with the idea of nationhood. What are we? Who are we? . . . What is it that stopped us from attaining the ideal?"[5] He saw the novel as an agent of change just as he saw American culture as a culture of change, so it should hardly surprise us that Ellison was concerned with politics in his novel writing. The more curious matter is his failure to address this matter fully in his work.

The political gestures of his characters are forever incomplete somehow. Ellison's invisible man promises to leave his hibernation and serve a socially responsible role. Yet in the context of the novel, he stays underground, seeming almost contented with what he claims Louis Armstrong would call "Old Bad Air." ("Old Bad Air is still around with his music and his dancing and his diversity, and I'll be up and around with mine.") Alonzo Hickman, or God's Trombone, from *Juneteenth* goes to Washington just as Martin Luther King, Jr., did, but he is there not to march or demand recognition, but to save the life of the bigoted, race-baiting Senator who was once his adopted son. This was the very man he had hoped would be an emissary for all African Americans. All of Ellison's major characters are speakers. From his cellar hole in Harlem, Ellison's invisible man describes himself as a former "rabble-rouser" and wonders if he will go back to raising rabble again. Alonzo Hickman is "God's Trombone," a preacher who at the right moment can find the word within the word. But his words never move outside of the insular world of the black church until his adopted son distorts and manipulates the techniques of God's trombone for his own ends. Then the techniques of the black church become the vehicle for racism. With those techniques, Bliss/Sunraider, who seeks in his speech on the Senate floor to crack the glass in the windows of the chamber, ultimately spews forth vitriolic racism until he is shot down in mid gesture. It is hard not to attach these seemingly incomplete political gestures to Ellison himself, in particular his incomplete novel.

Ellison himself seemed to promise in the acceptance speech that he gave for the 1952 National Book Award and later in his aforementioned reply to Irving Howe that he would write more novels. He stated in that speech that American culture was at a point of crisis and that it was the novelist's job to make readers aware of that crisis. In writing *Invisible Man* he had taken, he argued, a measure of "personal moral responsibility for democracy." Since in the same speech he referred to *Invisible Man* as his "not quite fully achieved attempt at a major novel," one could only expect more novels, perhaps a major novel. One could only expect that they would continue to assert a kind of moral responsibility for democracy.[6] But forty-two years later, there was still only one novel and the enormous unfinished manuscript of the next—the ultimate incomplete gesture. Coupled with Ellison's failure to be politically active, these incomplete gestures ultimately lead us back to the question of politics. If Ellison chose not to be political in his private life, did he also try, almost despite himself, to blunt or remove the politics from his novels? Was he that private a man, one who wanted to create art in a cloister? Or do we misread the politics of his novel because we expect of him, as so many of his colleagues did, an overt political involvement that is somehow unfair?

Complete answers to many of these questions will never be found. In some respects, the answers escaped us when Ellison died. In other respects, he might not have known the answers himself. Still, in seeking answers to these questions, we come face to face with a man who lived his life trying to be a novelist in a time when it was extraordinarily difficult for a black man to dream of such a career. So in his success and in his failure, he has much to teach us. But more than that, Ellison sought to be and became an American novelist of the first order. Thus, in his very public struggle with the form, in his countless essays that attempt somehow to probe into the heart of novel writing, we come face to face with the American novel itself. In many respects, as an American Ralph Ellison lived the question "What is the novel?" In interrogating what he left for us, we move closer to understanding Ralph Ellison's work and thereby the American novel itself.

Notes

1. "Ralph Ellison," prod. Avon Kirkland, *American Masters*, Public Broadcasting Corporation, February 2002.

2. John Callahan, "Introduction," *Juneteenth* (New York: Vintage, 1999), xxi.

3. Ralph Ellison, "The World and the Jug," The *Collected Essays of Ralph Ellison*, ed. John Callahan (New York: Modern Library, 1995), 188.

4. Ellison's use of this term is rather complex. I quote from a summary of a question-and-answer session that occurred at Lafayette College on April 18, 1969. The summary was compiled by Jon Reitman and is part of the Ellison collection at the Library of Congress. "When speaking of Negro traditions he [Ralph Ellison] preferred to use the term 'Negro American idiom' instead of 'black,' since the latter doesn't allow for enough geographical variation. In addition, the term Afro-American is culturally inaccurate, for in order to be correct he would have to identify himself with a particular African tribe (e.g., Ibo-American). He said the cultural term 'Negro American' evokes the emotions of the blues and spirituals, which go beyond color conflicts; he concluded, however, that when it is used in a political context, the term Black American is perfectly acceptable." Ralph Ellison Manuscripts, Library of Congress, box 174, folder 1. The title of this collection will be abbreviated as follows in future notes: REM, LOC.

5. Ellison, "The Novel as a Function of American Democracy," *The Collected Essays of Ralph Ellison*, ed. John Callahan (New York: Modern Library, 1995), 756. The title of this collection will be abbreviated in subsequent entries as *TCERE*.

6. Ellison, "Brave Words for a Startling Occasion," *TCERE*, 151.

Chapter One

The Invisible Man in Ralph Ellison's
Invisible Man

"Who knows but that, on the lower frequencies, I speak for you?"— Ralph Ellison, *Invisible Man*

The apocalyptic ending to Ralph Ellison's *Invisible Man* is nothing if not startling. Still, among all of the alarming moments in this ending, there is one that stands out for sheer absurdity. The narrator casts a spear at his long-time nemesis Ras the Exhorter, who has recently evolved to Ras the Destroyer. As the spear rips through both cheeks, it locks shut Ras's jaws. The narrator describes the scene in these unforgettable terms: "I let fly the spear and it was as though for a moment I had surrendered my life and begun to live again, watching it catch him as he turned his head to shout, ripping through both cheeks, and saw the surprised pause of the crowd as Ras wrestled with the spear that locked his jaws."[1] Even a casual reader is hard pressed to ignore the importance of this scene. The narrator seems to gain his long-sought moment of transcendence, finds his life in losing it, and reaches the end of his quest (the burden of his tale) in an act of violence. But it is an act of violence that partakes of the absurd. Only in cartoons do spears work so well or so conveniently to silence their victims, particularly when the spear caster is in such peril. Ras has called for the execution of the narrator: "'hang him!'" (559).

Clearly, we as readers are at an important juncture in the text: as the main character's life hangs in the balance, a spear locking the jaws of his rival seems to set him free by creating silence.

There are many ways to read this incident. Ras is the last of a series of father figures that the narrator has had to confront, understand, and escape. M. K. Singleton, among other critics, has detailed the repeated patterns of influence and rebellion that characterize the novel.[2] Starting with Booker T. Washington, evoked in the narrator's speech at the Battle Royal and continuing through Mr. Norton, Homer Barbee, Dr. Bledsoe, Mr. Emerson, Lucious Brockway, and Brother Jack and the Brotherhood, the narrator falls under the influence of one leader after another, only to rebel. Ras is the last of these figures, the representative of African nationalism who stalks him through the streets of Harlem as a rival speaker, accusing the narrator of faithlessness to the black man, seeking to align him with the ultimate father/mother symbol: Africa. When the narrator spears Ras with a part of Ras's own outlandish outfit, he is free, having found his life by losing it. Thus, he has lived out the prophetic words of the vet from the Golden Day: "'be your own father, young man'"(156). In the prologue and the epilogue, both of which take place outside of the context of the main events of the novel, we see a narrator who has become his own father, who has shaken off the restraints of a culture that cannot see him, a narrator who has achieved at least some measure of freedom.

Despite the appeal of its symmetry, such a reading ignores two important points: the similarity between Ras and the narrator and the manner in which the narrator silences Ras. Though he has been thrown into a leadership position in the novel, the narrator has actually not consciously sought to lead politically. Rather, he has sought success in general, a way to exercise his skill as a public speaker[3] and in so doing he has been pushed into the position of political leader. Most of his speaking in Harlem has been on behalf of the Brotherhood, an organization that hopes to use, even sacrifice, the black community to further its own revolutionary agenda. Though this fact is unknown to the narrator until late in the novel, the relatively lucrative salary, clothing, and office accommodations that association with the Brotherhood brings entice the narrator into being their voice in Harlem, even to the point of allowing them to script his speaking style.[4] These traditional trappings of American success have drawn the narrator in rather than the more spiritual/political search for black identity that seems to motivate a man like Ras. The narrator has been unwittingly the instrument of manipulating the black community.

Thus, garish as it is, Ras's costume is less outlandish than the invisible narrator's various embodiments as a speaker in the novel—from his bloody speech before the white men at the Battle Royal to his weeping before the audience at his first Brotherhood speech. Ras and the narrator are charlatans of the same order; they live by manipulating audiences with the oldest snake oil in the business: rhetoric. The narrator wants an American vision of success; Ras wants to return to the womb of Africa, taking his black brothers and sisters with him. But both of them are professional speakers, political candidates who seek the black vote.

Still, as Ellison's narrator tells us while ruminating on a portrait of Frederick Douglass in the Harlem office of the Brotherhood, "there was a magic in spoken words" (381). Thus, despite the fact that the narrator is drawn into the role of Brotherhood speaker out of a desire to find lucrative employment, a desire to exercise his skills as a speaker, the "magic" of language ultimately creates a relationship between him and the audiences to whom he speaks, a relationship that is transformed, perhaps even ruptured, in the spearing of Ras. In fact, after his first Brotherhood speech, the narrator feels drawn to and committed to the audience in a way quite different from how he feels drawn to and committed to the Brotherhood. His commitment to the Brotherhood is motivated by ambition, even greed: "I saw no limits, it was the one organization in the whole country in which I could reach the very top and I meant to get there" (380). But his connection to the audience is more seminal: "I felt a kind of affection for the blurred audience whose faces I had never clearly seen. They had been with me from the first word. . . . I had spoken for them, and they had recognized my words. I belonged to them" (353). If the narrator is opportunistic in his use of the Brotherhood (just as they are in their use of him), he is quite different in his approach to the audience. To them he feels committed, not by money or ambition, but by the intrinsic demands of truth.

Though this new reading of the scene places the issue of speech at the very center of the novel, the skeptical reader should note that in much of Ellison's mature work, speech is a vital issue. The narrator of *Invisible Man* clearly sees himself as a speaker when he alludes to "my talent for public speaking" (298) or when he describes himself in the Prologue as "an orator and a rabble rouser" (14) or when he agrees to become a professional speaker on behalf of the Brotherhood. What is more, a significant portion of the text of *Invisible Man* is devoted to describing and analyzing the narrator's speeches, which he delivers at the Battle Royal, at the eviction in Harlem, at various Brotherhood gatherings, or at Tod

Clifton's funeral in Harlem. Even the speeches of others, such as that of Blind Homer Barbee, are described in great detail. Finally, in the posthumous *Juneteenth,* a portion of a book that Ellison spent much of his mature life attempting to complete, speech is also at center stage. Not only are the main characters (one a politician, the other a minister) professional speakers, but also, as in *Invisible Man,* the text of the novel itself focuses upon speeches. The opening chapters give us verbatim Senator Sunraider's speech on the floor of the Senate. Sunraider has learned to speak from Hickman, so much so that Hickman recognizes in Sunraider's congressional speech techniques that he has taught him.[5] Finally, as Hickman talks with the dying Sunraider, a sizable portion of their conversation recounts the life of an evangelist, a man who spreads God's message word by word. Certain chapters are almost entirely given over to recounting speeches: chapter two of *Juneteenth* gives us verbatim Senator Sunraider's speech on the floor of the Senate prior to his being shot. What is more, as Hickman and Sunraider uncover the past, they are consistently drawn into remembering sermons. Chapter six is a recounting of the creation story in sermon form with constant references to a famed preacher called Eatmore. Chapter seven is a recapitulation of the call and response sermon that Bliss and Hickman delivered. Thus, the emphasis on speech that we find in *Invisible Man* seems hardly unique to that novel. Given the attention that Ellison seems to grant to speech in his work as a novelist, it should not surprise us to find it at center stage in the climactic closing scene in *Invisible Man* when the narrator's spear locks the jaws of Ras, his rival speaker in Harlem. Thus, the task of understanding this scene becomes vitally important, perhaps even pivotal, in understanding the novel itself. Further, I contend that understanding the role of language, in terms of both speech and writing, plays a major role in understanding Ellison's work as a whole.

In locking the jaws of his rival, the narrator is actually locking his own jaws. By so doing, he is liberated, saved from a role that has become intolerable. "I had surrendered my life and begun to live again" (560), he tells us. Importantly, the role that has become intolerable is not only the role of Brotherhood representative but also the role of speaker. As the narrator says just before this pivotal spear hurling, "But even as I spoke I knew it was no good. I had no words and no eloquence" (558). Ironically, notwithstanding the title of the novel, speech has brought to the narrator a kind of visibility. In the context of such an understanding of the novel, the narrator's trip underground is more than an attempt to rediscover himself or finally become his own father. Rather, it is a flight from speech, which has brought him visibility, to writing, a new mode of expression, that brings with it invisibility. Ras is a very visible speaker in Harlem. With his outlandish costume, he cannot be missed. Despite the many levels on which he is invisible as a black man in a white man's world, the narrator, like Ras, is recognizable in Harlem when he speaks. In fact, even in the turmoil of a riot-torn night in Harlem, Ras sees and recognizes the narrator.

What is more, the narrator's whole career quite literally begins when he becomes visible as a speaker. Brother Jack watches him deliver an impromptu protest speech at a Harlem eviction. As he speaks for the Brotherhood, it is the organization's hope that he will be visible as a black man, thereby swaying others in their behalf. Even when he discovers late in the novel the trick of slipping into the identity of Rinehart by putting on dark glasses, he is still visible as Rinehart. Only in going underground to write does the narrator truly become the invisible man of the novel's title. Thus, invisibility is a many-faceted metaphor in this novel. The title of the novel implies that the narrator is invisible to white people because he is black. White people refuse to see black people. But I contend that in another sense only by being invisible can the narrator escape the visible embodiment of what he has become, only by the invisibility of writing can he overcome the visibility of speech. What is more, when the novel is finished, invisibility is a condition not only of the narrator but also of all people and of Ellison himself.

There is no point in *Invisible Man* when we see the narrator engaged in the act of writing. Nonetheless, in many respects the novel foregrounds the written text as a phase of the narrator's life qualitatively different from his life as a speaker, the life he describes in his story. It is the embodiment of what he becomes after the events of the novel, the fruit of the underground, the story of his life told in retrospect, from the standpoint of invisibility underground. It is quite literally the only means for him to understand and articulate his aboveground experience. The narrator's words in the prologue express this fact: "Could this compulsion to put invisibility down in black and white be thus an urge to make music of invisibility? But I am an orator, a rabble-rouser—Am? I *was,* and perhaps shall be again. Who knows?" (14). We do not know as we read the novel whether the text will be that which propels the narrator to speak again or that which substitutes for speaking. As Yonka Kristeva argues in "Chaos and Pattern in Ellison's *Invisible Man,*" "Ellison focuses on a liminal state, a process of transition and becoming which is unresolved at

the end of the novel."[6] We do know, however, the underground has enabled the narrator "to put invisibility down in black and white."

Several statements from Ellison himself suggest that writing has become an important part of the circle of the narrator's experience, perhaps
even more important than the events the novel describes. He told one
interviewer, "The epilogue was necessary to complete the action begun
when he [the narrator] set out to write his memoirs."[7] At another point in
the same interview Ellison suggests that the narrator does become visible
again through the vehicle of writing: "The hero comes up from underground because the act of writing and thinking necessitated it."[8] In another interview Ellison says "he comes out of the ground, and this can be
seen when you realize that although *Invisible Man* is my novel, it is
really his memoir."[9] Thus, the novel, or "memoir" as Ellison calls it, may
be understood as the narrator's path out of the underground. Paradoxically, as irony begins to pile on irony, the very act of writing invisibly
gives the narrator a way of becoming visible to an audience of readers
whereas speech was done visibly but necessitated his invisibility.

Complicating the matter still further, Ellison speaks in these quotations of an event that never occurs in the novel. In actuality, the narrator
never leaves the underground. He implies that he will, that it will be a
part of the next phase, but in the text of the novel he never separates himself from the underground.[10] Ellison clearly assumes that he will leave
and even ties that act to writing, saying, "the act of writing and thinking
necessitated it" or "the epilogue was necessary to complete the action
begun when he [the narrator] set out to write his memoirs." Thus, writing
assumes quite a significant role. It is not only the narrator's way out of
the underground, but also, in Ellison's eyes, it points toward the completion of an action that is in actuality never completed in the novel. Understanding these ironies and complications that are here unearthed forces
the reader to explore writing as a facet of this novel and subsequently of
Ellison's work as a whole. However, since writing is never directly a part
of the action in *Invisible Man* or any other Ellison work, our best route to
understanding it is to explore its relationship to its alter ego: speech.
Given its prominence as a form of African-American art and the ways in
which it appears and reappears in Ellison's work, speech deserves more
attention than most Ellison critics have accorded it. My first task will be
to address this failure. But I wish to do more than examine speakers and
speeches in Ellison's work. My hope is to grasp at least some of the ways
in which Ellison understood writing and his role as a black writer in
twentieth-century America. After all, while he wrote, American life was

changed forever by the speeches of Dr. Martin Luther King, Jr., a man who perfected the very art that Ellison's narrator seems at least for a time to reject. All the while, Ellison himself remained essentially invisible, working on a novel that he never finished.

Ellison is certainly not the first writer to suggest that speech is in profound ways different from writing. In fact, any careful reading of the history of rhetoric, indeed the history of Western literature and philosophy, demonstrates that speaking and writing have been understood as vastly different ways of communicating. I do not argue here that Ellison alludes in any way to the history of rhetoric or to any other specific interpretation of the differences in speech and writing. I argue only that in making his main character "an orator, a rabble rouser" who becomes a writer on the way to evolving into some new entity, Ellison invites us to consider some of the differences between the two.

Fifth-century Athens is generally known as the birthplace of rhetoric in the Western world, the place where the first serious discussions of this issue occurred. Most of the public use of language in that culture was speaking. In fact, the writing that the sophists and other teachers of rhetoric undertook was primarily to write speeches for hire or to teach students to become proficient at writing their own speeches: the assumed media of language was the spoken, not the written, word. Two of Plato's dialogues deal directly with the subject of rhetoric. In the earlier dialogue, the *Gorgias*, Socrates tells Gorgias, a well-known speaker, rhetorician, and sophist from Sicily, that rhetoric is a branch of flattery. When asked if it is a base or a fine thing, Socrates unequivocally calls it "base."[11] Even in the later dialogue, the *Phaedrus*, which scholars tend to agree is more favorable toward rhetoric,[12] Socrates makes the job of the speaker one requiring almost superhuman skill and endeavor: "He who is to be a rhetorician must know the various forms of the soul."[13] Later in the same dialogue Socrates argues that the path of rhetorical skill is a long one and should not be undertaken to please men but to please the gods: "Therefore, if the path be long, be not astonished; for it must be trodden for great end."[14] One wonders whether any mere mortal is capable of being a rhetorician if the requirements are so intense. On the other hand, in the same dialogue Socrates comes very close to ridiculing writing when he tells Phaedrus that words sown by a pen "cannot defend themselves by argument and cannot teach the truth effectively."[15] Phaedrus calls the written word "an image" of the "living and breathing word of him who knows." [16]

Much of what we are presented as speech in *Invisible Man* suggests that Ellison's narrator discovers, as Socrates argues in the *Gorgias*, that rhetoric as it is embodied in speech is "a base thing." What is more, never in the course of *Invisible Man* do we see the narrator treading the path of speaker for the great end of pleasing the gods or any other divine entity. Rather, he is interested in pleasing men, all too often the wrong men. On the other hand, contrary to Plato, Ellison seems to grant to writing a higher position, one that prefigures Jacques Derrida's rethinking of the relationship between speaking and writing in the last half of the twentieth century.

Still, important aspects of the tradition of speech and writing stand closer in time to Ellison than to Plato. Though the foundations of classical rhetoric are evident everywhere in our culture, there were no sermons in ancient Athens, and there were no novels. Each of these forms profoundly colors the perception of both speech and writing in *Invisible Man*. Ellison's own particular experience with writing and with speech clearly involved the novel and the sermon. Furthermore, by the time he wrote *Invisible Man* he had also heard many political speeches. Thus, any examination of the issues of speech and writing in Ellison's work must examine the role that these three forms play in Ellison's work. Ellison was, after all, a novelist, and a novelist who took quite seriously the task of speaking out on the role of the novel in American culture and Western history. His two collections of essays, *Shadow and Act* and *Going to the Territory,* give us ample evidence of this fact.[17] What is more, Ellison almost certainly heard more sermons and political speeches than any other types of speech. Both of these forms are reenacted in *Invisible Man* and in *Juneteenth*. Our concern here will be first to explore Ellison's use of speech in his work. Later, in a separate chapter, we will delve into the other half of the issue, namely, his understanding of and use of the role of the novel.

Ellison was named for Ralph Waldo Emerson, the grand man of American letters during the first half of the nineteenth century, who also happened to be a defrocked minister who became an essayist and a poet and arguably the most important speaker during the first half of the nineteenth century in the United States.[18] What is more, after Ellison's father (who chose the name in the hope that his son would become a poet) died when his son Ralph was only three, Ellison's mother, Ida, worked as stewardess of the Avery Chapel Afro-Methodist Episcopal church.[19] Since the minister had a home of his own, the widow and her sons even lived in the parsonage where the young Ralph Waldo read books that were left in the house by the minister.[20] It is quite likely that most of the early speeches that Ellison heard were sermons and that his understanding of speech was in large part shaped by the sermonic form. The overpowering figure of Alonzo Hickman in *Juneteenth* would certainly underscore that fact.

The speeches Ellison heard while a student at Tuskegee Institute were probably quite similar in form. Mark Busby explains in *Ralph Ellison* that Homer Barbee's speech in *Invisible Man* was likely modeled on an actual speech delivered in chapel at Tuskegee Institute while Ellison was a student. Major Robert Moton, president of the college, delivered an oration during the fall of Ellison's freshman year in which he described a dying Booker T. Washington summoning Moton to his bedside and saying "'Major, don't forget Tuskegee.'"[21] The fact that Ellison the writer remembers this incident more than ten years later, giving to his character Homer Barbee a similar incident in a fictional chapel speech, suggests that Ellison had more than a cursory understanding of the power of pulpit oratory. After all, when he heard the speech, he was not a writer at all. Rather, he was studying to be a musician.

Though Ellison might not have heard political speeches as frequently as he heard sermons, by the time he wrote *Invisible Man* he was doubtlessly quite familiar with the form. In "The Rhetoric of Anticommunism in *Invisible Man*," Barbara Foley argues that Ellison's connections to the American Communist Party during the forties were much closer than most people have assumed. In fact, she states that until the end of the war, "Ellison hewed to the Communist Party line."[22] She also contends that Ellison repudiated such stances in *Invisible Man* by indulging in what she calls anticommunist Cold War rhetoric. Such an argument (not to mention Ellison's well-known connections to Richard Wright and Ellison's writing for Communist Party publications) makes highly likely the idea that Ellison very much had the political speeches he had heard in mind when he wrote *Invisible Man.*

Critics have often tied *Invisible Man* to the rich heritage of music that Ellison knew and absorbed as a young man growing up in an African-American community, as a young man educated in music at an African-American college. Far fewer critics have tied the novel to the equally rich oral tradition that it clearly grows out of. [23] Despite this fact, there is ample evidence to support the existence of such influences not only in Ellison's past but also in the work itself. Still, before exploring the speeches we find in *Invisible Man,* we must understand some of the basic qualities of the oral traditions that Ellison explores in both of his novels.

One of the most distinctive qualities of the sermon when placed in the context of other oratory is its adherence to a particular text. George Kennedy explains this distinction in his history of rhetoric: "The classical orator had a free field in choice of a proposition and the topics for proving it. He used or invented arguments from many sources. . . . The primary function of the Christian orator, in contrast, was to interpret and bring into practice the holy word."[24] A second point is implied here. As an oratorical midwife, bringing to life scripture, the minister's role is essentially passive; as Kennedy says later in the same passage, the minister's job is to create "'a projection of the eloquence of scripture.'"[25] Thus, whatever eloquence may be a part of the final product should find its source in the text of scripture and not in the speaker. In his history of preaching, Yngve Brilioth attributes to Augustine's *De Doctrina Christiana* the notion that "the sermon is basically the exposition of a text."[26] What is more, calling Augustine's book the first attempt to write "a homiletics," Brilioth states that in the sermon, oratory "is the humble servant of wisdom."[27] Both of these discussions recall for us the classical distinction of the two roles of rhetoric drawn by Socrates as "a branch of flattery" and as a means for finding and conveying truth. Implicit here is the notion that the minister who sticks to the text conveys truth, and the minister who indulges in eloquence outside of that provided by the text is somehow illegitimately seeking flattery. Ministers should not seek beautiful words in themselves or as a means to impress their audiences. Rather, the minister allows the beautiful words of the text to shine through his or her sermon. Still, applying such observations wholesale to the black pulpit oratory Ellison experienced and re-creates in his novels is a tricky proposition. In fact, the distance between this classical definition of the sermon and the sermons that we see in Ellison's work illuminates for us some of the distinctive qualities of the black sermon.

In his book *The Sermon and the African American Literary Imagination* Dolan Hubbard argues that "Christian explanations" have never adequately or fully explained black oratory or the black church because they fail to account for the large impact of oral and folk traditions on the black world.[28] What is more, according to Hubbard, the black sermon is focused primarily on two effects: the proclamation of black freedom and the creation of a communal sense of catharsis, releasing the audience not only from domination by white folks but also from what Hubbard calls "the tyranny of the everyday."[29] According to Hubbard, the road to both of these effects is not rational persuasion, which he associates with the Euro-American sermon, but "authoritative proclamation and joyful celebration."[30] Implied in this explanation of black pulpit oratory is the celebration of both individuality and community. The minister proclaims the word out of his authority, his adherence to the text not only of the Bible but also of black life. But in this authoritative proclamation the minister brings to life not just the text but also the communal catharsis of his audience. It is for this reason that the "call and response" pattern of black pulpit oratory is so important. Thus, whereas in traditional pulpit oratory, the minister allows the text of scripture to speak with its own eloquence and by so doing is in many respects midwife to the sacred text which he or she had no part in constructing, in the black pulpit, the speaker is interested in giving to the audience a communal voice, in creating the possibility of self-definition through community articulation. Looking back again at Plato's discussion of rhetoric, one may conclude that the African-American sermon plays havoc with Plato's carefully honed distinction between rhetoric as a kind of flattery, a matter of sound and not sense, and rhetoric as a tool for finding and conveying truth. The black sermon conveys a kind of truth that involves not just the text or the truth, but also a kind of play with language that the call and response tradition celebrates. In fact, one might almost argue that the minister finds his text in what goes on between him or her and the audience.

When we place these distinctions into the context of Kennedy's comments quoted above concerning preaching in general, we notice another important distinction between black pulpit oratory and pulpit oratory in general. The black preacher is much more likely than the Euro-American preacher to bring the Bible to life specifically as it applies to black people. Accordingly, Hubbard argues "'Let my people go' is the most responsive mascon in the peculiar eschatology of the black church."[31] Hubbard also maintains that in the black church the minister is clearly focused on God's role in history, in particular, God's role in bringing freedom to black people. As Hubbard argues, "The Israelites victory is transformed into black victory."[32] To Hubbard, the preacher "defines freedom as the ability to articulate the self."[33] Since he stands before the audience and does this not as an individual but as a man who is collectively speaking for the whole community, he allows the audience to define itself through his articulation of its needs. The center of these needs for most of the twentieth century was the liberation of black people from the tyranny of white prejudice and the poison of white assumptions. Clearly, the black minister goes far beyond the literal text of the scripture to achieve his task while the European minister is one who simply allows the text to speak. Rather than being a kind of midwife, delivering unto the congregation the text that he or she was handed, the black minister becomes the burning center of communal transformation.

Two speeches in *Invisible Man* clearly fall into the tradition I have set forth here: the sermon the narrator dreams of in the prologue to the novel on the "Blackness of blackness" and Homer Barbee's speech in the chapel at the narrator's college. But before we can examine these speeches, we must understand the basic form of the political speeches that we encounter in *Invisible Man*. In at least some respects these speeches give us the opposite pole of speech in the novel, the speech as a tool of community conformity rather than community articulation, speech that ironically resembles Kennedy's definition of the European sermon: the delivering of a text.

Political speech is not nearly so easy to define as the sermon, for it is a much looser category. Earlier I quoted Kennedy's comments concerning the sermon: the preacher is limited to the text of the Bible or the religious tradition to prove a point, whereas the classical rhetorician has a free field of reference. Political speakers would fall in this broader category; ostensibly they adhere to no prescribed text. A political speech may be any oral presentation that sets forth a proposal of a political position, particularly one in which the speaker hopes to influence others. For example, Senator Sunraider's speech on the floor of the Senate in *Juneteenth* in which he advocates changing the name of the Cadillac to the "Coon Cage Eight" is a political speech.[34] He hopes to move those in his audience to understand his political position and even adopt it insofar as they accept and enact his proposal. In his *Rhetoric* Aristotle sets forth a category for political speech when he divides rhetoric into three groups: deliberative, forensic, and epideictic speech.[35] Political speech falls into the first category and is distinguished from the other two by its time orientation. Unlike forensic rhetoric that focuses on the past and epideictic rhetoric that focuses on the present, deliberative rhetoric focuses on the future. Its intent is always to shape policy. The speaker who uses forensic speech hopes to establish guilt or innocence in a legal setting based on examination of the past, whereas the speaker who uses epideictic speech celebrates a particular event or occasion in the here and now.

Still, Aristotle's categories are only useful insofar as they retain a kind of looseness. For example, though the sermon fits into the broad category of celebratory or epideictic rhetoric, we may also observe that at least some sermons seek to effect policy change or even indict someone or some organization that might be antithetical to the aims of Christianity or of the Christian community, or perhaps even the community in general. By the same token, the political speech, which is deliberative in form, might also invoke some sort of celebration. Dr. Martin Luther King, Jr.'s "I Have a Dream Speech" set forth a policy agenda, but it also celebrated the American ideal of freedom as it indicted the country as a whole for failing to live up to the opening lines of the Declaration of Independence. King's speech clearly partakes of all three of the categories that Aristotle sets forth. Hubbard's observation that "'Let my people go' is the most responsive mascon in the peculiar eschatology of the black church"[36] suggests a sermon form that falls somewhere between deliberation of policy and celebration of community. It is also clearly an indictment of white America, tying it to the image of the Egyptians in the Old Testament who enslaved the Israelites. Despite the looseness and the mixing of these categories, this basic distinction will be very important to our understanding of Ellison's work: the black sermon celebrates and liberates through celebration and articulation, whereas the political speech sets forth policy. The latter is much more a matter of logic, while the former invokes emotion as the partner of logic. Indeed on some occasions, emotion becomes the doorway to understanding.

Just as we see sermons in *Invisible Man*, we also see political speeches: the narrator's attempts to speak as representative of the Brotherhood are in every case political speeches. In fact, the narrator's first Brotherhood speech delineates for us the distinctions set forth above between the black sermon and the political speech. Whereas the narrator and the audience seem very much attuned to each other in this speech, the Brotherhood finds the audience involvement troubling. During the speech itself, an audience member screams out that the narrator is "batting .500" (345) in his speech, and the narrator responds to the audience, "I feel, I feel suddenly . . . *more human*" (346). The narrator even weeps before the audience. But the Brotherhood assessment of the speech attacks it on the grounds of its emotionalism, the very grounds of what would seem to be its success. One brother describes the speech as "wild, hysterical, politically irresponsible and dangerous," (349) whereas another calls it "the antithesis of the scientific approach" (351). Accordingly, the Brotherhood officially silences the narrator, so that he can be "trained." The Brotherhood's understanding of political speech rejects the emotionalism of the narrator's first attempt. Indeed, whatever articulation of community needs that the Brotherhood desires is to be carefully scripted, imposed from without rather than discovered and articulated in the give-and-take between the audience and the speaker. It is a "text," we might conclude, to which the narrator must adhere.

I began this chapter with the image of the narrator of *Invisible Man* locking shut Ras the Destroyer's jaws with a spear. Thereby, I argued that the narrator finds new life by silencing not only Ras but also himself: "I had surrendered my life and begun to live again," (560) he tells us. In silencing himself the narrator moves from the visibility of speech to the invisibility of writing. Paradoxically, the hopes that he expresses in the prologue and epilogue suggest that writing will bring him a kind of self-definition that speech has denied him, that his novel or his "memoirs" as Ellison calls them, will ultimately allow him to step out of the underground and assume a role as a visible man influencing a visible audience.[37] Thus, it would seem that speech is rejected in *Invisible Man* as an idiom of transformation, perhaps even as a vehicle of community articulation. But as with so much else that we find in Ellison, these conclusions may be tenuous. Though the narrator of *Invisible Man* does indeed become a writer, it is as a speaker that we know him best, for that is his role in most of the story he writes. Thus, it is not quite as easy as we might expect to dismiss speech or to understand fully the transformation of the narrator. We are left with questions, with loose ends.

If speech is rejected as a mode of self or community definition in *Invisible Man*, why does Ellison put before the reader the many forms of speech that his narrator encounters? Why does the narrator hint in the prologue that he may indeed become a speaker again, claiming still to be a speaker?[38] Such devices show us that Ellison's own understanding of the culture of which he writes places speech in a position of great importance, defining not only the individual but also the community. Despite these facts, the narrator, a self-confessed "rabble rouser" with "a talent for public speaking," chooses to go underground and write, producing a document that Ellison himself would later call the "memoirs" of the narrator. In similar fashion, Ellison would define himself as a writer, even going so far in his famous written exchange with Irving Howe as to claim writing as his role in the Civil Rights movement.[39] But after the 1952 publication of *Invisible Man* Ellison was a writer who worked for the rest of his life (some forty-four years) on a novel he never finished. What is more, that novel in part chronicled the death and in some respects the life of another speaker, a political speaker who learned political speech from a black preacher, a black preacher who presides over his death. In addition, during at least a portion of this time, the very ground underneath Ellison's feet was being shifted by the sermons of Martin

Luther King, Jr., and the actions that those sermons inspired, by the speeches of Malcolm X and the subsequent Black Power movement, both movements that Ellison remained aloof from in any active sense of involvement. With such a welter of images and counter images of speech and speakers, writers and writing, in both the writing and the world of Ralph Ellison, many questions come to mind. My task here will be to phrase these and with luck answer at least a few of them.

Notes

1. Ralph Ellison, *Invisible Man,* 2nd ed. (New York: Vintage, 1995), 559-60. All references are to this edition and appear parenthetically within the text. The abbreviation IM only appears within the parenthetical listing if the context of the quotation does not establish to which of Ellison's novels I am referring.

2. Many articles argue this position. Among the most interesting are these:

M. K. Singleton, "Leadership Mirages as Antagonists in *Invisible Man*," in *Twentieth Century Interpretations of Invisible Man*, ed. John M. Riley (Englewood Cliffs, N.J.: Prentice Hall, 1970).

Robert B. Stepto, "Literacy and Hibernation: Ralph Ellison's *Invisible Man*," in *Ralph Ellison: Modern Critical Views,* ed. Harold Bloom (New Haven, Conn.: Chelsea House, 1986).

3. The narrator observes "It was, after all, a job that promised to exercise my talent for public speaking" (298).

4. The narrator initially refuses to work for Brother Jack. Then he changes his mind, seeking him out because, "if the pay was anything at all it would be more than I had now" (298). His initial reaction to his new salary is "Sixty a week!" (310). Clearly, money is an important factor in his decision.

5. Hickman observes, "Imagine, going up there to New England and using all that kind of old Southern stuff, our own stuff, which we never get a chance to use on a broad platform—and making it pay off," Ralph Ellison, *Juneteenth*, ed. John Callahan (New York: Vintage, 1999), 35.

6. Yonka Kristeva, "Chaos and Pattern in Ellison's *Invisible Man*," *Southern Literary Journal* 30, no. 4 (fall 1997): 68.

7. Ralph Ellison, "The Art of Fiction: An Interview," TCERE, 219.

8. Ellison, "The Art of Fiction," *TCERE*, 220.

9. Ralph Ellison, "On Initiation Rites and Power," *TCERE*, 537.

10. Understanding the narrator's comments on this matter is in itself difficult. On the last page of the novel, he states, "Thus, having tried to give pattern to the chaos which lives within the pattern of your certainties, I must come out, I must emerge. And there's still a conflict within me. With Louis Armstrong one

half of me says, 'Open the window and let the foul air out,' while the other says 'It's good green corn before the harvest.' Of course Louis was kidding, *he* wouldn't have thrown old Bad Air out, because it would have broken up the music and the dance, when it was the good music that came from the bell of old Bad Air's horn that counted" (581). These words suggest at least that the underground is the only context that makes the music of the novel possible.

11. Plato, *Gorgias*, in *Readings in Classical Rhetoric*, Ed. Thomas W. Benson and Michael H. Prosser, trans. W. R. M. Lamb. (Davis, Calif.: Hermagoras Press, 1988), 19.

12. Eric Segal, "Introduction," *The Dialogues of Plato* (New York: Bantam, 1986), *X*.

13. Plato, *Phaedrus*, in *Readings in Classical Rhetoric,* Ed. Thomas W. Benson and Michael H. Prosser, trans. H. N. Fowler (Davis, Calif.: Hermagoras Press, 1988), 35.

14. Plato, *Phaedrus*, 37.

15. Ibid., 39.

16. Ibid., 24.

17. Ellison writes: "The novel was not invented by an American, nor even for Americans, but we are a people who have perhaps most need of it—a form which can produce imaginative models of the total society if the individual writer has the imagination, and can endow each character, scene and punctuation mark with his own sense of value." Ralph Ellison, "The Novel as a Function of American Democracy," *TCERE*, 764.

18. Reverend Hickman discusses Emerson with Bliss in this passage from *Juneteenth*: "I guess it's 'bout time I started reading some Shakespeare and Emerson. Yes, it's about time. Who's Emerson? He was a preacher too, Bliss, just like you. He wrote a heap of stuff and he was what is called a *philosopher.* Main thing though is that he knew that every tub has to sit on its own bottom. Have you remembered the rest of the sermon I taught you?" Ralph Ellison, *Juneteenth*, Ed. John Callahan (New York: Vintage, 1999), 45.

19. Ellison writes in a letter to Albert Murray dated July 24, 1953, concerning a trip home, "The sad thing about it, of course, was that so many were missing: my mother and father (who I learned used to say that he was raising me for a poet! Poor man.)" Quoted from Albert Murray and John Callahan, *Trading Twelves: The Selected Letters of Ralph Ellison and Albert Murray* (New York: Modern Library, 2000), 43.

20. Lawrence Jackson, *Ralph Ellison: Emergence of Genius* (New York: John Wiley and Sons, 2001), 26.

21. Mark Busby, *Ralph Ellison* (New York: Twayne, 1991), 7.

22. Barbara Foley, "The Rhetoric of Anticommunism in Invisible Man," *College English* 59 (1997): 9.

23. Notable exceptions here would be Dolan Hubbard's discussion of *Invisible Man* in his *The Sermon and the African American Literary Tradition*.

24. George A. Kennedy, *Classical Rhetoric and Its Christian and Secular Tradition from Ancient to Modern Times* (Chapel Hill: University of North Carolina Press, 1980), 137.

25. Ibid.

26. Yngve Brilioth, *A Brief History of Preaching*, trans. Karl E. Mattson (Philadelphia: Fortress, 1965), 50.

27. Ibid.

28. Dolan Hubbard, *The Sermon and the African American Literary Imagination* (Columbia: University of Missouri Press, 1994), 19.

29. Ibid., 24.

30. Ibid., 17.

31. Ibid., 83.

32. Ibid.

33. Ibid., 5.

34. Sunraider states: "I am led to suggest, and quite seriously, that legislation be drawn up to rename it the 'Coon Cage Eight.' And not at all because of its eight super efficient cylinders, nor because of the lean springing strength and beauty of its general outlines. Not at all, but because it has now become such a common sight to see eight or more of our darker brethren crowded together enjoying its power." Ralph Ellison, *Juneteenth*, Ed. John Callahan (New York: Vintage, 1999), 23.

35. Aristotle, *The Art of Rhetoric*, trans. H. C. Lawson-Tancred (New York: Penguin, 1991), 80-81.

36. Hubbard, 83.

37. "Perhaps that's my greatest social crime, I've overstayed my hibernation, since there's a possibility that even an invisible man has a socially responsible role to play" (581).

38. "But I am an orator, a rabble rouser—Am, I was and perhaps shall be again" (14).

39. At the end of "The World and the Jug," Ellison states: "Dear Irving, I am still yakking on and there's many a thousand gone, but I assure that no Negroes are beating down my door, putting pressure on me to join the Negro Freedom Movement, for the simple reason that they realize that I am enlisted for the duration. . . . For, you see, my Negro friends recognize a certain division of labor among the members of the tribe. Their demands, like that of many whites, are that I publish more novels—and here I am remiss and vulnerable, perhaps." Ralph Ellison, "The World and the Jug," *TCERE*, 187-88.

Chapter Two

The Magic and the Mystery of Words

"In the beginning was not only the word, but its contradiction."
—Ralph Ellison, "Society, Morality, and the Novel"

From the black minister's speech in the prologue on the "Blackness of Blackness" to the narrator's speech at the Battle Royal to the narrator's speech at the funeral of Tod Clifton to the narrator's final words to Ras the Detroyer, speaking is a major pattern of action in *Invisible Man*. What is more, many of the speeches dramatically illustrate the most sacred and deep-seated of the narrator's motivations and the rank absurdity of the context in which he is forced to express them. Finally, in almost every case in the novel, speech accomplishes nothing, this despite Ellison's careful exploration of the form. Thus, as I argued in chapter one, the novel dramatically embodies the narrator's gradual transformation from speaker to writer.[1] Despite this transformation, in the end we are left with a narrator who is somewhere between writer and speaker and an audience that is without a voice. Even as early as the narrator's speech at the Battle Royal the narrator starts the process of evolving from speaker to writer by beginning to unravel the nature of public speech.

Not only is the audience at the Battle Royal a group of drunken white men who have just subjected the narrator and his friends to a racist, sexist carnival of lust, blood, and wanton brutality, but also the narrator himself bases his speech upon Booker T. Washington's *Atlanta Exposi-*

tion Address. Very much in the tradition of the European sermon discussed in chapter one, the narrator has a text, and he presents it, allowing the text to speak through him. What is more, his text is a well-known document in the history of American culture. Washington's speech is just the type of speech that white audiences like,[2] one that suggests no changes or discontent of any kind. Ironically, as if to underscore this point and to introduce the ambiguous nature of language and speechmaking, Ellison has his narrator misspeak, so that he says "social equality" for "social responsibility." This failure to follow the text emphasizes the importance of the narrator's relationship to Washington and those whom we might associate with Washington's point of view. Washington was well known and well liked among whites because he did not ask for social equality.[3] Thus, the narrator's failure to follow the text on this particular point sets off a minor furor in the all-white audience. Only when the narrator is corrected and returns to the prepared text can the audience relax to hear the rest of his speech.

Ironically, despite the latent hostility in the audience and the questionable nature of the text of the speech, we as readers should see something else very significant in this speech: the narrator's ardor and sincerity. As he tells us amid his description of boxing blindfolded among his peers, "I wanted to deliver my speech more than anything in the world, because I felt that only these men could truly judge my ability" (25). To grasp fully the significance of this statement, we as readers must remind ourselves of the context. Ellison's narrator stands amid a group of inattentive, drunken bigots, he speaks a speech based upon a text of questionable value to African Americans, but he speaks with ardor and sincerity. As the novel progresses, speaking or writing, the narrator does not lose his desire to be understood. His last words in the narrative (those of a writer now and not a speaker) express something of the same desire to an audience of readers, some of whom are black and some of whom are white: "Who knows but that, on the lower frequencies, I speak for you?" (581). The narrator's speech at the Battle Royal thus begins the process of unraveling the narrator's attempts to communicate with an audience, a process that will continue through the end of the novel. The desire to be understood is the center of the narrator's motivation (thus, the desire to speak and later to write, "torturing myself to put it down" [579]), yet the art of speechmaking repeatedly forces the narrator to become something he is not, ultimately making him visible as a speaker but invisible as a voice. Further, his ultimate failure to communicate leaves both him and his audience in need.

Throughout the novel, the speeches the narrator delivers tend to reiterate these points, but increasingly Ellison forces us as readers to become enmeshed within the complexities of rhetoric and politics. The first speech the narrator delivers in the North during the second half of the novel grows again out of a sincere desire to be heard. As the narrator sees a mob protesting an eviction on the streets of Harlem, he tells us, " I saw them start up the steps and felt suddenly as though my head would split" (275). The narrator's response is immediate and spontaneous: "there boiled up all the shock-absorbing phrases that I had learned all my life" (275). Again, the narrator has a text to follow, words that he has "learned," just as he had learned the words of Booker T. Washington. But it is important to note that the narrator is to some extent aware of the deceptiveness of that text. He tells us that he "seemed to totter on the edge of a great dark hole" (275), that he both wants and does not want the impending violence that his speech and his "shock-absorbing" words will forestall. In fact, "the shock-absorbing phrases" are a response to his fear of "what the sight of violence might release in me" (275). Thus, though he speaks to forestall the violence, he knows that the violence itself speaks to something deep inside him.

The speech is then an attempt to manipulate the audience, to keep it from doing what it inevitably does anyway, what the speaker himself feels drawn to, namely, riot. It is, to quote Socrates, "a base thing," if we consider deception in this situation to be base. What is more, technique becomes an important issue in the narrator's attempt to communicate. As his first approach fails, the narrator observes, "Oh, God, this wasn't it at all. Poor techniques and not at all what I intended" (276). He flounders through another more successful phase, describing the age of the couple being evicted, the sanctity of their belongings, strewn along the streets. But not until he adopts a word that the audience hands him does he begin to hit his stride. "'Dispossessed?' I cried, holding up my hand and allowing the word to whistle from my throat. 'That's a good word, 'Dispossessed'! 'Dispossessed,' eighty-seven years and dispossessed of what? They aint *got* nothing, they caint *get* nothing, they never *had* nothing. So who was dispossessed?" (279). What begins to develop with this word is a communal explanation of what has happened. The narrator begins to preach in words articulated on the spot in a communal exchange between himself and the audience. He deserts the text with which he came into the situation. Thus, unlike the speech the narrator delivers at the Battle Royal, which reflects Booker T. Washington, the eviction speech reflects the oral traditions of the African-American church, traditions that suggest communication, sharing between the audience and the speaker. What is more, unlike the speech at the Battle Royal, during which the audience is preoccupied and inattentive ("But still they talked and still they laughed, as though deaf with cotton in dirty ears" [30].), the audience at the eviction becomes involved in what the narrator says. He is aware of them as an audience with a need to hear what he says: "Let's follow a leader, let's organize. *Organize*" (276), he tells them. An audience member responds to the narrator in the style of a member of a church congregation: "Tell 'em about it, brother" (279). Still, despite the narrator's momentary success, the riot that was beginning when the narrator interrupted ensues, and the narrator ultimately flees. As in the case of the speech at the Battle Royal, the narrator accomplishes nothing. In fact, since he feels drawn toward the violence he sees fermenting in the crowd, in some respects he deserts the very audience with whom he has identified.

This speech differs in important ways from the speech at the Battle Royal. First, it is participatory in the sense that the narrator abandons the learned text, "the shock-absorbing phrases," and the audience in part supplies the words that evolve. Second, just as the narrator is aware of his position as speaker, of his potential to manipulate the audience, the narrator is also aware of the audience's need for a leader. In the speech at the Battle Royal the narrator speaks "automatically and with such fervor that I did not realize that the men were still talking and laughing until my dry mouth, filling up with blood from the cut, almost strangled me" (30). Such is not the case at the eviction. The narrator drops the automatic words for words supplied by the audience, and the narrator recognizes the audience as a group of people in need.

Ironically, though this speech has no effect on the riot and in that sense is a failure, it does make the narrator visible to Brother Jack. Thus, this speech, delivered extemporaneously and with sincere feeling, partaking for a moment of the call and response tradition of the black church, propels the narrator into the sharply defined role of speaker that he only escapes when he hurls the spear at Ras. Talking to the narrator after he (the narrator) has fled the scene of the riot, Jack observes that the narrator has been "well trained," compliments him on his "eloquence." Finally, he asks him, "How would you like to be the new Booker T. Washington?" (305). Since this question reminds us of the narrator's speech at the Battle Royal, since Washington was the most widely recognized black political leader in the United States prior to Martin Luther King, Jr., it has enormous significance to the theme of this study. The narrator is being asked to assume the role of a speaker, but more specifically the mantle of a black politician who was known to be a practiced manipulator. What is more, though the narrator argues that the Founder was greater than Booker T. Washington, he ultimately agrees to fulfill the role that the Brotherhood has for him.[4] In fact, in case a reader misses the connection between Washington and the narrator, Ellison makes it painfully clear in Brother Jack's subsequent words: "So it isn't a matter of whether you wish to be the new Booker T. Washington, my friend. Booker Washington was resurrected today at a certain eviction in Harlem" (307). This statement suggests a kind of inevitability. The narrator *is* Booker T. Washington, whether he wants to be or not; any black man who stands up and speaks assumes the role of Booker T. If we tie this suggestion to the sermon tradition described in chapter one, in the style of the European minister, the narrator has a text of a sort, ready and waiting, supplied by the Brotherhood. The narrator's first speech for the Brotherhood further underscores this point,[5] but not without again enmeshing us in the complications of rhetoric and politics.

In his first Brotherhood speech, the narrator speaks from a position of physical isolation that reflects the psychological isolation of the Brotherhood. On a deeper level this isolation reflects Washington's isolation from the true dilemmas of African-American life. On a still deeper level, it reflects the narrator's isolation from what Socrates calls the "great end" of speech, pleasing the gods. As in the Battle Royal speech in which the narrator sought to please the white town fathers, the narrator is now seeking to please the men of the Brotherhood and not the gods. None of this should surprise us, for the narrator is speaking from the resurrected body of Booker T. Washington. Thus, he cannot see the audience; they are "the bowl of human faces" (341). The microphone is "strange and unnerving." The narrator confesses to the audience that he has not "learned the technique" of speaking into a microphone. Still, ironically, the narrator breaks through these contextual barriers to the audience. In his earlier speech at the Harlem eviction, the word "dispossession" becomes the link between the narrator and the audience; here Ellison introduces a new metaphor. An audience member shouts "We with you, Brother. You pitch 'em we catch 'em." As the narrator speaks, the anonymous audience member calls strikes, finally saying, "you don't pitch no balls" (344).

This aspect of the speech reflects the eviction speech. The analogy of pitch and catch embodies the call and response tradition of the black church in a metaphor that any audience member can grasp and identify with. What is more, once again, the audience is giving the speaker a line, giving him a connection, even a technique that will allow him to become a part of the communal experience of speech. He will not explain to them the dilemma of African Americans in the community. Together audience and speaker will articulate the issues. As in the eviction speech, the narrator also becomes aware of the audience's need for leadership: "I'll look out for you, and you look out for me!" (344), the narrator tells the audience. At the end of the speech there is a kind of catharsis, much in the style that Dolan Hubbard attributes to the black sermon.[6] The narrator claims to have undergone *"Something strange and miraculous and transforming"* (italics in original). In putting this experience into words, he is speechless, almost in the same way that one who has been transformed by a spiritual experience might find himself or herself at a loss for words: "I stumbled in a stillness so complete that I could hear the gears of the huge clock." (346). Later as red spots dance before his eyes, he claims to stumble in "a game of blindman's bluff" (347), recalling for us his boxing blindfolded at the Battle Royal as well as Blind Barbee.

I pointed out in chapter one that Socrates argues that the speaker should seek to please the gods. This speech in many respects accomplishes that end despite the artificially constructed context in which it exists, despite the narrator's Brotherhood-scripted role as Booker T. Washington. It transforms both the audience and the narrator into a spiritual state. As a consequence, for the Brotherhood this speech is potentially dangerous. Brother Jack walks up to the narrator during the speech and warns, "Don't end your usefulness before you've begun" (345). After the speech, the "brother with the pipe" summarizes the general consensus of the group: "the new brother must learn to speak scientifically. He must be trained" (351). The Brotherhood is concerned with the matter of how closely the speech adheres to the standard that they have set forth, the text, one might argue, that they have for the speech. If we place this comment into the context of Brother Jack's statement after the eviction, we recognize that, though the narrator has become the resurrected Booker T. Washington, he has once again failed to adhere to the text—he has slipped in his lines just as he did at the Battle Royal. As in that speech, he must be corrected.

In many respects this speech brings together all that we have discovered about speech thus far in the novel. It reiterates the promise and the betrayal of both speaker and audience in the context of speechmaking. The narrator is carrying a message for the white folks. But ironically, through the presence of the audience, he begins to speak for himself and for them. His tears at the end of the speech confirm once again the sincerity of his convictions as well as the potential of the speaker/audience relationship to transform lives. In the speech at the Battle Royal, delivering the speech is the most important of his goals; here, when he stands before the audience, his tears suggest again the importance of his speech. They suggest his ardor and sincerity. But in the context of the sham that the Brotherhood is perpetrating, these tears become as absurd as Ras's outlandish outfit. They are embarrassing to the narrator.

Still, ironically, the audience and the speaker are both in need. The audience needs to commune with someone who can see, who can guide it. As the narrator says, "We share a common dispossession" (345). They lack a voice, and despite the artificiality of his situation, the narrator seeks to give them one: it is a voice that can evolve only in their presence, a voice that comes from them. Thus, the narrator's bewildered, unexpected cry at the end of the speech—*"I have become more human"*—is indeed true (italics in original). But at this particular moment, the voice the narrator uses is his own, not that of the resurrected Booker T. Washington. Therefore, the Brotherhood must restore the text.

Recognizing the need for leadership inherent in this situation is an important part of understanding the dilemma that Ellison confronts in this novel. Ellison stated in another of his many interviews, "I was concerned with the nature of leadership, and thus with the nature of the hero, precisely because during the historical moment when I was working out the concept of *Invisible Man* my people were involved in a terrific quarrel with the federal government."[7] Lawrence Jackson reports that as early as 1945 when Ellison applied for a Rosenwald Fellowship, he was planning a novel on black leadership.[8] By casting his main character into the role of potential leader of his people in the tradition of Booker T. Washington, Ellison is confronting a question that was of vital importance to the American community in 1952: who will speak for the black community, the invisible face of American culture? Current readers of *Invisible Man* have a difficult time recognizing the full significance of that question in 1952, for since then Martin Luther King, Jr., and the Civil Rights movement have changed radically the political landscape of the United States. In 1952, there was no organized, nationally recognized Civil Rights movement. Martin Luther King, Jr., was an obscure Baptist minister in Montgomery, Alabama. The bus boycotts (which would take place in Montgomery), the opening volley of the Civil Rights movement, were four years in the future. The NAACP, founded in 1909 by W. E. B. Du Bois, was certainly an organization that fought for the rights of people of African descent. However, the organization suffered a substantial defeat in 1946 and 1947 when it boldly approached the newly formed United Nations with a "Petition to the United Nations on Behalf of Thirteen Million Oppressed Negro citizens of America." In 1946 the petition was ignored, and in 1947 it was rejected by the delegation from the United States. Though the Soviet members of the UN's Commission on Human Rights endorsed the petition, such meager support brought no redress for the grievances that formed the center of the petition. NAACP leaders like Du Bois were reduced to the tactic of waging war quietly through protest and court cases (thus Thurgood Marshall's famous victory before the U. S. Supreme Court in *Brown v. Board of Education of Topeka, Kansas* in 1954, two years after the publication of *Invisible Man*). A look at the actions of black leaders of the day reveals just how hopeless and fragmented these actions might have seemed.

Du Bois split with the NAACP in 1948 because of politics—Walter White, the executive secretary, supported Truman for President while Du Bois supported Henry Wallace of the Progressive Party. Du Bois's future was filled with what might be called a gradual retreat from the mainstream of American life. Indicted and later acquitted in 1951 as a subversive, in 1961 he officially joined the Communist Party. By the time he died in 1963, he had given up on citizenship in the United States, becoming a full citizen of Ghana, a true African at last.

Ellison's longtime friend and mentor, Richard Wright, had come to conclusions similar to those of Du Bois much earlier, choosing to live in France, a permanent expatriate. Ralph Bunche, who in 1950 became the first African American to win the Nobel Peace Prize, was a government bureaucrat who worked tirelessly for the rights of Israel and was instrumental in the founding of the UN. Martin Luther King, Jr., won the Nobel Peace Prize in 1963 because of his actions on behalf of African Americans; Ralph Bunche won the prize in 1950 because of his efforts to broker peace in the Middle East. And though Bunche was certainly well-known as a leader of African Americans, his positions often put him at odds with the NAACP. Brian Urquhart explains in his *Ralph Bunche: An American Life*: "Although race and racism were an essential element of the problems of Black Americans, Bunche believed at this time [the 1930s] it was a mistake to assume that their problems were basically racial in nature. Most of their problems, he felt, stemmed from the wider failure to improve the standard of living of the working class."[9] Given his views, it is not hard to see how Bunche might have earned a reputation for being at odds with most of the African-American leaders of his day, especially W. E. B. Du Bois and the NAACP.

Other figures attest further to the incoherence of African-American politics of the day. Adam Clayton Powell, Jr., was probably the most well known and widely recognized political leader of the day. Arriving in Congress representing the Harlem District of New York City in 1945, Powell was called "the Negro chosen by destiny."[10] And he was able to boast many accomplishments during his long tenure in Congress. But he was unable to do anything about the poverty of the very community he served. What is more, he himself refused to live in Harlem and pursued a life style that most African Americans would have had great trouble identifying with. Biographer Wil Haygood notes that Powell was a "peripatetic" politician, accused of "chronic absenteeism" because of his constant travel: "He undertook his trips at times on behalf of committee work, and at other times for the sheer pursuit of pleasure. Powell would not take a back seat to liberal, Dixiecrat or hedonist."[11] Married to the beautiful, talented African-American musician Hazel Scott, Powell was light-skinned and quite handsome, the son of Adam Clayton Powell, Sr., the famed former minister of the Abyssinian Baptist Church in Harlem. He stood up for the rights of African Americans, but many of his most celebrated positions had a distinctly upper-class quality and seemed almost doomed to frustrate what might have been his wider effectiveness.

When the Daughters of the American Revolution refused to allow his wife to perform at Constitution Hall in Washington, D.C., Powell immediately sent a telegram to President Truman: "'Request immediate action on your part in the situation of my wife Hazel Scott concert pianist being barred from Constitution Hall because she is a Negro.'"[12] Not only did Truman turn down Powell's request, stating that the organization was private and none of his affair, but also Truman's wife, a DAR member, continued her membership in the organization despite Powell's protest. In 1946 when Truman threw a party for the entire 80th Congress, Powell was the only member not invited. According to Haygood, "Truman never forgot Powell's attack on his wife, and as long as he remained President he prevented Powell from entering the White House."[13] Often at odds with the NAACP as well as the administration, Powell lived the life of a dandy, frequenting the nicest bars in Harlem in the company of socialites like Franklin Roosevelt, Jr. Thus, despite his effectiveness as a politician, he was certainly not the type of leader of the people that the narrator of *Invisible Man* aspires to be. What is more, he was not the kind of leader who would change the character of African-American life in this country. Therefore, Ellison, as he wrote *Invisible Man*, had good reason to consider African Americans in this country to be a people without a political voice, a people who were invisible. Consequently, it should not be surprising that the narrator wishes to fill the vacuum, to prove himself as a leader who can make a difference in the lives of the people in his audience. Thus, though the narrator may have accepted his role within the Brotherhood as a way of collecting a salary, though he may have sought to rise in the Brotherhood in an attempt to embody the classic American success story, he is moved by the audiences he encounters.

In his first speech for the Brotherhood, the narrator feels empowered to lead. After he returns home from his first Brotherhood speech, accepting as necessary the training under Hambro that the Brotherhood demands in order to make him speak more "scientifically," he marvels at the words he has spoken, thinking alternately, "Already it seemed the expression of someone else," then "Yet I knew that it was mine and mine alone" (353). But the two images that haunt him most are the phrase, "more human" and "a kind of affection for the blurred audience whose faces I had never clearly seen. . . . I would do whatever was necessary to serve them well" (353). The narrator is committed to the audience. Further, like the narrator's first speech, this oration underscores for us the important qualities of speech in *Invisible Man*: the ambiguous nature of speech, but also the narrator's ultimate sincerity, and the audience's desperate need. The scripted words—what we might call the words of the resurrected Booker T. Washington—move the narrator away from the audience while the words the audience provides move him toward them.

In many respects, the "training" that the Brotherhood supplies has unintended consequences, for though the narrator masters the "science" of brotherhood and becomes quite successful as a speaker in Harlem, his Brotherhood experience ultimately leads him also to reject the organization and at least for a time, speaking itself. The forces that drive him away from the Brotherhood and from speech come together when he offers his last official speech at the funeral of Tod Clifton as well as when he spears Ras the Exhorter. But before we can understand the importance of this speech or that incident (with which chapter one started), we must examine the narrator's interaction with Brother Tarp and his subsequent transformation. Brother Jack insists that the narrator is the resurrected Booker T. Washington. Tarp, on the other hand, introduces into the narrator's official Brotherhood world another important African-American speaker, Frederick Douglass. Both Robert Stepto and M. K. Singleton have explored extensively and fruitfully the relationship between the narrator and Washington and Douglass, but neither has noticed the way in which Ellison's use of these historical figures bears directly upon the issues of speech and writing in the novel.

Though a relatively minor character in the novel, Tarp's role is pivotal in understanding the transformation of the narrator from speaker to writer. As the narrator moves into his Harlem office after his Brotherhood-imposed training period, Tarp shows the narrator his office. On the narrator's first morning on the job, he passes along to him a portrait of Frederick Douglass. Whereas Brother Jack insisted that the narrator was the resurrection of Booker T. Washington, Tarp's words concerning Douglass are much less constrictive. The narrator confesses to knowing little about Douglass, and Tarp responds, "That's enough. He was a great man. You just take a look at him once in a while" (378). When the narrator thanks Tarp for the portrait, Tarp responds, "Don't thank me, son, ... He belongs to all of us" (378). Despite the unrestrictive terms upon which the narrator is granted this gift, the narrator is constantly aware of the Douglass portrait throughout his successful period of work with the Brotherhood, what he calls "those days of certainty" (380). But in what is perhaps his most important confrontation with the portrait, the narrator compares himself to Douglass, a comparison that should remind us of the parallels that Brother Jack draws between the narrator and Booker T. Washington:

> For now I had begun to believe, despite all the talk of science around me, that there was a magic in spoken words. Sometimes I sat watching the watery play of light upon Douglass' portrait, thinking how magical it was that he had talked his way from slavery to a government ministry and so swiftly. Perhaps, I thought, something of the kind is happening to me. (381)

This rumination upon Douglass ultimately revolves around speaking, for the narrator sees in himself something of the same speaking ability that Douglass used—"Well, I had made a speech, and it had made me a leader" (381). Further, the narrator ties his own uncharted transformation to what he remembers from the life of Douglass.

The contrast here is very important. Brother Jack gives the narrator no choice but to become the resurrected Booker T. Washington. When the narrator speaks on behalf of the Brotherhood, he is expected to follow the "scientific" point of view of the Brotherhood, namely, the text. Tarp gives the narrator the Douglass portrait only as a guide, a guide that is in a sense from the audience itself ("He belongs to all of us"). The narrator himself recognizes in the example of Douglass a kind of refusal to follow the text: Douglass's transformation from slave to speaker to writer was uncharted, improvised, partaking in large part of the unknown and the unplanned, a desertion of the text. Given this important contrast between these two figures and their relationship to the narrator, Ellison invites the reader to contemplate Douglass not as a model for the narrator but as a model for the possibility of the power of words, what the narrator calls the "magic" of words.

Like the narrator, Douglass came North seeking something other than the life of an orator or a leader. Douglass sought work in the shipyards; the narrator sought work in general with his letters of recommendation from Dr. Bledsoe. Like the narrator, Douglass got a new name (his real name was Frederick Bailey) in the North when he became an orator. Finally, Douglass was the narrator's grandfather's great hero. In fact, the Douglass portrait reminds the narrator of his grandfather's comments about another orator whose name was transformed as he changed identities: Paul of Tarsus. According to the narrator's grandfather, "You start Saul, and end up Paul, ...When you're a youngun, you Saul, but let life whup your head a bit and you starts to trying to be Paul—though you still Sauls around on the side" (381). Bringing Paul of Tarsus into this complicated comparison underscores again the importance of language.[14]

Like Douglass and the narrator, Paul traveled away from home with one motive in mind and wound up transformed in the direction of another motive. As Douglass went from being a shipyard worker to being an orator and an abolitionist, so Paul went from being a persecutor of Christians to being an advocate of Christians. In fact, he became the most vocal advocate that Christianity had in its early period. Finally, both Paul and Douglass were speaker/writers who were faced with audiences of various ethnic groups. Douglass's task as a part of the Abolitionist Movement was to convince white citizens that African Americans were their equals, that slavery was inhuman. He did this through his powerful speaking on behalf of the Abolitionist Movement and other causes, but he also accomplished recognition for his position through his eloquent writing. Similarly Paul dropped a Jewish name in ceasing to be Saul, and a large part of his mission involved the spreading of Christianity beyond the Jewish world, to the Gentiles. Like Douglass, Paul traveled and spoke, but also, like Douglass, he wrote. The letters of Paul are a major component of the New Testament, just as Douglass's writing has become a major component of world and American literature as well as world and American history. Both Paul and Douglass were writers whose writing transformed the world around them. In fact, Douglass's writing did more than establish the inhumanity of slavery or the equality of Africans and Europeans. According to Patricia Liggins Hill's *Call and Response*, Douglass was "one of the first people to propose that slavery was a failure of the imagination, a failure, in other words, to create new visions of humanity since the European Renaissance."[15] In similar fashion, Paul wrote not a narrative of the life of Christ; rather, he explained the emerging religion of Christianity to itself. His thinking became the philosophical underpinning of the Christian movement. Thus, in the context of *Invisible Man* both Douglass and Paul of Tarsus become counterexamples to Booker T. Washington. Whereas Washington accommodated himself to white audiences, accommodated himself to the text of the day one might argue, Douglass and Paul transformed their audiences with the "magic" of words, audiences that were often hostile. Whereas Washington was a writer whose books were largely ghost written,[16] Douglass and Paul were writers whose powerful imaginations transformed the way in which their readers viewed the world. Whereas Brother Jack gives the narrator Booker T. Washington and the science of Brotherhood to the narrator as models that he should follow slavishly, Tarp gives the narrator the Douglass portrait as a reminder, a reminder of someone who belongs to all people of African descent. It is as if Tarp is giving the narrator a forgotten part of the narrator's self.

The symmetry of these comparisons tempts one to assume that the narrator exchanges the Booker T. Washington persona provided for him by the Brotherhood for the Frederick Douglass persona, that in becoming a writer, he becomes a latter-day Frederick Douglass. But such a reading misses the rich complexity of Ellison's novel. In the previous chapter I cited Yonka Kisteva's statement that *Invisible Man* is about a man in "a liminal state."[17] Such an observation is well worth remembering at this point. We do not ultimately get to understand and experience the complete transformation that the narrator undergoes. Whether Saul does ultimately become Paul or whether Booker T. eventually morphs into a latter-day Frederick Douglass who will lead his people, we do not know, for we leave the narrator at the end of the novel contemplating the process of coming out of hibernation. Furthermore, the Douglass portrait that he reflects upon is soon lost. As association with the Brotherhood brings him into contact with Tarp and the portrait of Douglass, so it severs him from both. Because of his interview with the so called "new picture magazine," the narrator invokes the wrath of Westrum and the suspicion of the entire Brotherhood. He is thus forced to become inactive in Harlem, sent outside of Harlem to speak on "the woman question."[18] When he returns to his old office, both the Douglass portrait and Tarp are gone. But the narrator does find Tod Clifton, and Tod Clifton's death becomes the context for the narrator's last speech, another of those uncharted transformations wrought by the "magic of words."

Tod Clifton's own transformation and subsequent death are two of the most important and confusing events within *Invisible Man*. His transformation is one of the book's great mysteries, for we never see the process of transformation, only the result. As Brotherhood representatives, he and the narrator together fight Ras on the streets of Harlem. Moreover, Clifton himself articulates for the narrator the only real explanation that is ever given for Clifton's transformation. In commenting on Ras, Clifton reasons, "I suppose sometimes a man *has* to plunge outside history" (377). Clifton adds to this what might be a foreshadowing of the narrator's trip underground to write: "Plunge outside, turn his back. . . . Otherwise he might kill somebody, go nuts" (377).

Other details of the narrative only add to the mystery of Tod Clifton. It is Clifton whom Ras calls a "black king" (373). Also, the narrator spits on Clifton's racist Sambo doll when he finds him selling Sambo dolls on the streets of Harlem, in part bringing on Clifton's arrest by the police. Finally, Clifton's spiel concerning Sambo employs a memorable word from both the narrator's eviction speech and his first Brotherhood speech. The doll becomes in many respects another gift akin to the portrait of Douglass in that it gives back to the narrator something of himself. But unlike the Douglass portrait, the Sambo doll tells the narrator facts about himself he would rather not know.

Fully unraveling the complexities of Clifton's transformation is impossible even for the narrator. Why would a man who is committed to changing his community become the purveyor of a racist symbol, even hoping to make money off such an item? Though it might be impossible to answer this question, the Sambo doll itself is one of a pattern of symbols in the book. Like the link from Tarp's chain or the bank from Mary Rambo's house, the Sambo doll ultimately carries a message for the narrator, becoming a part of the briefcase that embodies, as Robert Stepto has effectively argued, the narrator's transformation (57). But the Sambo doll is more important than any of those other items in a study such as this one, for it becomes a vital part of preparing both the reader and the narrator for the oration at the funeral for Tod Clifton and his subsequent transformation into a writer. The Sambo doll dancing on the sidewalk is finally a speaker in two senses. First, he speaks to the narrator and, second, he embodies the narrator.

Given the fact that the doll's name is Sambo, it is not surprising that he embodies many of the white stereotypes of African Americans: like a minstrel he dances, he makes his audience laugh, and he seems indestructible ("Shake him, shake him, you cannot break him" [432]). But two of the statements that Clifton makes about the Sambo doll reflect the narrator's association with the Brotherhood: *he'll kill your depression and your dispossession*" (432) and, *"And only twenty-five cents, the brotherly two bits of a dollar"* (italics in original) (433). Since the narrator has sought for himself and his people (those faces in the audience whom he has committed himself to) a way to kill dispossession, we can view the Sambo doll as an emblem of the narrator. Like Sambo, the narrator seems virtually indestructible. He has indeed been shaken and pushed around within the Brotherhood and he has made his audiences laugh—and all for money, *"the brotherly two bits of a dollar"* (433). This last phrase suggests the Brotherhood, not only since Ellison uses the term *"brotherly,"* but also because one member of the Brotherhood is named "Tobitt."[19] Thus, it cannot be totally surprising that in coming to terms with the mystery of Clifton's death, the narrator begins to have important doubts about himself, particularly his involvement with the Brotherhood: "My breath became short; I felt myself go weak. What if he [Clifton] believed I'd sold out?. . . I sat holding myself as if I might break" (447). Ironically, as the narrator thinks these thoughts, he is holding the Sambo doll. So energetic, limber, and agreeable, the doll for just an instant reminds the narrator of himself in his relationship to the Brotherhood.[20] And just as Frederick Douglass's transformation took him far beyond the Abolitionist movement where he began, so the narrator begins to define himself in such a way that he severs his connection to the Brotherhood.

Still, once again, Ellison is very much aware of the subtlety of consciousness; the narrator's transformation is gradual. The narrator does not rise up and walk away from the Brotherhood. Rather, he evolves away from the stranglehold that it has upon his mind and his voice, so that at the end of the novel he is a writer and not a speaker; he is in hibernation, not leading a revolution or a riot. The pivotal step in this process, however, is once again speech. In the absence of contact with the Brotherhood, the narrator decides that he must single-handedly plan a funeral for Clifton. The reasons for this funeral are those that we might expect from a Sambo doll—the narrator wants to ingratiate himself with the Brotherhood's leadership by making the most of Clifton's death: "I seized upon the idea now as though it would save my life. . . . We had to use every politically effective weapon against them; Clifton understood that" (447-48). So once again, the narrator seeks to manipulate the audience, to use those who will attend the funeral for a political end, to use Clifton's death itself (even his body) for a political end. In similar fashion despite his moments of sincerity and inspiration, he has always used his audiences to advance himself, to advance the Brotherhood. And in this case as in the others, it is what happens in the context of the audience that transforms him and that ultimately leaves him speechless.

The narrator's eulogy leads us as readers directly to the spear that locks Ras's jaw and to the novel or memoir writer that the narrator becomes. Like Homer Barbee's speech earlier in the novel, the narrator's last formal speech eulogizes a fallen leader, but unlike that speaker, the narrator does not claim for himself or the object of his eulogy transcendence, nor does he reach toward the transcendence that he stumbles upon at the first Brotherhood speech. Ultimately, he offers no absolution to the silent audience. He even eschews the whole notion of technique that has been essential to every speech he has offered thus far. This speech, unlike all of the others, claims nothing for itself, not even the eloquence that the narrator has long cherished and that attracted the notice of Brother Jack. What is more, this speech introduces us to a tone we have not heard before in any of the narrator's speeches, a tone of sarcasm and irony that will characterize the prologue and epilogue.

Before the audience at the Battle Royal, before the audience at the Harlem eviction, before the audience at the first Brotherhood speech, the narrator has been motivated to speak. At the funeral of Todd Clifton, the narrator is "nudged" and begins to speak what he calls "final words." He speaks again as the spokesperson for the Brotherhood. But for the first time in the novel, he has no text of any sort, whether it be a model speech, such as the *Atlanta Exposition Address*, or a set of expectations, such as those that he learns to cater to as a representative of the Brotherhood. He confesses not to understand how a Brotherhood funeral should be handled: "I stood there alone; there was no microphone to support me, only the coffin before me upon the backs of its wobbly carpenter's horses" (454). He begins with a sincere confession of inadequacy: "what are you waiting for me to tell you?" (454). What is more, he rejects the role of the preacher, the role we have seen him move toward in his previous Brotherhood speeches, the role that might tie him to Homer Barbee or to the call and response tradition that inspires him in earlier Brotherhood speeches: "Go home, he's as dead as he'll ever die. That's the end in the beginning and there's no encore. There'll be no miracles and there's no one here to preach a sermon." (454-55). He is reduced to fact only. Repeating "What are you waiting for me to tell you?" (454) and "Go home, forget him" (455) and "What are you waiting for, when all I can tell you is his name?" (455), the narrator denies any claim to transcendence, such as one might expect in a traditional eulogy or a sermon in the black church: "And don't be fooled, for these bones shall not rise again" (458). The narrator does not even find any reason to grant Clifton any earthly transcendence, such as one might expect in a politician eulogizing a fallen martyr. Tod Clifton will not live on among them in spirit: "Go take a drink and forget it" he tells the audience. In fact, the ultimate summation of the event is filled with a kind of sarcasm that reduces the event to black comedy: "It [the killing of Tod Clifton] was perfectly natural. The blood ran like blood in a comic-book killing, on a comic book street in a comic book town on a comic book day in a comic book world" (457-58). In his first Brotherhood speech the narrator wept because he felt more human. In this speech, he goes to the opposite extreme: he deprives his subject of humanity, turning him into a comic book character. He also denies to the audience the ultimate human response of tears. "Take a drink," he suggests.

The narrator's rhetorical strategy is that of understatement and sarcasm. It proceeds by indirection: the serious is treated without seriousness; the sacred is profaned. However, though the narrator's view of the audience is in many respects clearer than it has been at any time before ("I saw not a crowd but the set face of individual men and women" [459]), the audience does not respond at all to his speech. As the narrator ceases to speak, claiming to be unable to go on, he recognizes the failure of his words: " I had let it get away from me, had been unable to bring in the political issues. And they stood there sun-beaten and sweat-bathed, listening to me repeat what was known" (459). In disavowing a rhetoric that operates through creating the possibility of transcendence, the narrator has lost his power to politicize the event. But he has also lost his power to move the audience.

This speech raises important questions. Can fact speak for itself, particularly in a novel in which the visible is unseen, a novel that begins with the line, "I am an invisible man" (3)? The narrator's earlier speeches (at least those to which the reader is privy) have ultimately refused to accept the dehumanizing effect of a culture in which the narrator and those like him are invisible. "I'll look out for you, and you look out for me!" (344), the narrator tells the audience at his first Brotherhood speech. In the context of such a statement, he feels *more human*, feels that he has undergone *"Something strange and miraculous and trans-forming"* (347). Even within the context of speaking for the Brotherhood, which is in many respects dehumanizing, the narrator and the audience have found their common humanity. He has in many respects become visible, at least in the context of the audience. But if Tod Clifton is only a comic book figure whose death matters no more than the next drink, can the narrator truly serve the audience he committed himself to earlier in the novel ("I would do whatever was necessary to serve them well" [353])? Has the narrator done any more than acknowledge what he does on the first page of the novel, the invisibility of human beings such as himself and Tod Clifton?

Moreover, when he sees the audience as individual men and women, has he lost his original vision of them as an audience that needs a leader? A writer writes to individuals who read his books silently and often alone. A speaker speaks to groups, galvanizing them into action, into something more powerful than that which individuals can be on their own. And though novels can create actions and motivate groups, just as speeches can, the dynamic is quite different. Action created by speech is more direct and immediate. As Socrates says, he who knows the truth will not "sow" words with the pen, for they "cannot defend themselves by argument."[21] Thus, the narrator's final speech is in many respects at least a temporary disavowal of the rhetoric of the speech, a rejection of the immediacy of speech. It also rejects the transcendence that we might associate with the sermonic tradition in the black church or the political speech, the transcendence that brings the narrator to tears at the end of his first Brotherhood speech. Further, in the context of such a disavowal, the speaker and the audience somehow part company. They are no longer a group that needs a leader; they are individuals. He is no longer a leader; he is just one more invisible man. He feels the tension that simmers in their midst, but is unable to dispel or direct it: "something had to be done before it simmered away in the heat" (461). In this context, the narrator's move underground becomes the ultimate trip toward invisibility. And the riot on the streets of Harlem becomes the embodiment of chaos, all members of the audience going in individual directions.

The narrator's eulogy over the fallen body of Tod Clifton takes on an added significance when we place it beside Homer Barbee's speech (a eulogy for the Founder) from earlier in the novel. Despite the fact that Barbee's speech is in the final analysis a sham, even the skeptical narrator (who is seeing it from the retrospective posture of the underground) is aware of its power. Blind Barbee's speech at the narrator's college clearly partakes of the sacred in the narrator's mind: "Here upon this stage the black rite of Horatio Alger was performed to God's own acting script. . . . Not the wafer and the wine, but the flesh and the blood, vibrant and alive" (111). The narrator implies an intense communion, one that goes beyond symbolism into true transubstantiation where blood and flesh mingle with blood and flesh. As Barbee moves from a third person rendition of the "Founder's life" to a second person collective reliving of the life ("You left with the Founder in the black of night" [122]), the audience is indeed consuming the transforming blood and wine of the Founder's life. The effect is so profound that the narrator remembers, "Blind Barbee had made me both feel my guilt and accept it" (134). Still, the narrator's subsequent experience belies the absolution this communion promises. Not only is the narrator punished for his sins by being expelled from the college (a kind of eternal damnation in his mind at the time), but also Dr. Bledsoe's (the Founder's hand-picked successor) damning letters of reference demonstrate that the whole foundation of the college is little more than a sham. Thus, the sacred desire for absolution collides with the absurdity of a world in which ritual is sham and even the power structures of the oppressed are corrupt. As the narrator speaks blindly to the audience at the Battle Royal, so Blind Barbee blindly leads the narrator into a world of mirrors in which the narrator's so-called sins are visible and the proffered absolution does nothing to wash them away. But he does lead, something that the narrator relinquishes at the end of the novel when he can summon only the facts in response to the murder of Tod Clifton.

Only in the context of this deflating of the rhetorical stance of the earlier speeches does the final confrontation with Ras make sense. Only in the context of such a deflating of the rhetorical stance of speech itself do the prologue and epilogue make sense. Only when there is nothing left to say does the speaker lock his own jaws and become a writer. Thus, in many respects, the narrator insists finally upon the very dispossession that he has complained about earlier in the novel: "WE'LL BE DISPOS-SESSED NO MORE!" (346), he tells the audience at his first Brotherhood speech. In transforming Tod Clifton, the so-called black king, into a comic book figure, the narrator removes from the audience the possibility of transcendence, the possibility that what he calls "the magic of words" provides. And while it is certainly true that the narrator's intent is to highlight these events by understatement, we hear fully evolved in this speech (and we see fully evolved in the person who throws the spear at Ras) the voice, the being, that will speak to us in the prologue and epilogue, in the novel itself, a voice of sarcasm and irony, a writer's words, not a speaker's voice. When we place these words into the context of the traditions of oratory that this novel has seemed to embrace, we recognize that Ellison is suggesting that in the world of 1952 Harlem, there is no room for the sincere voice of the young man who tells us while slugging his brothers, "I wanted to deliver my speech more than anything in the world" (25) or who weeps before an audience that has somehow resurrected him, the exhumed Booker T. Washington. Perhaps in such a world there is no place for the preacher's voice, the voice we hear echoed in Homer Barbee early in the novel and picked up by the narrator in his brotherhood speeches.

We must remember again that Ellison was concerned in this novel with the nature of leadership: "I was very much involved with the question of just why our Negro leadership was never able to enforce its will."[22] The fact that the narrator at least temporarily gives up on his quest to lead is significant. The spearing of Ras becomes the active embodiment of what happens rhetorically in the narrator's last speech: the rejection of speech and the politics of speech. Ras is thus an important character both politically and rhetorically because he recklessly continues to pursue what the narrator abandons. He is the reductio ad absurdum of the narrator's rhetorical self, as comic and surreal as the narrator's image from his eulogy for Tod Clifton: "a comic-book killing, on a comic book street in a comic book town on a comic book day in a comic book world" (457-58). As such, we must look at the important historical association that Ras brings into the novel.

As pointed out earlier, Singleton and Stepto as well as other critics have examined the historical figures and the father figures who are exhumed, examined, and rejected in the course of this novel. But one of the ironies that has not been carefully examined or explained is the curious absence of contemporary figures in Ellison's gallery of allusions. Certainly, the Brotherhood does have important parallels to the American Communist Party of the thirties and forties, but most of the figures alluded to in *Invisible Man* were prominent in African-American politics long before its 1952 publication date. Ras is certainly one of these, for in his embodiment of African nationalism, he seems to echo Marcus Garvey, prominent in Harlem during the twenties. Significantly diminished in influence during the thirties, Garvey died in 1940. Garvey was not an African American. He was from Jamaica. Though we never know the origin of Ras, his dialect tends to suggest that he is West Indian in origin. What is more, his Afro-centric message as well as his military pomp suggests Garvey.

Garvey is an interesting figure in the history of African-American leaders in this country and certainly one who would cross the mind of a writer interested in questioning the accomplishments of black leadership in the twentieth century. A precursor in many respects to the leaders of the Black Power movement of the sixties and seventies, Garvey initially championed the success ethic of Booker T. Washington against the more intellectually oriented positions of W. E. B. Du Bois. Garvey parodied the NAACP, which Du Bois founded, by calling it the "National Association for the Advancement of Certain People."[23] Garvey's own organization, the Universal Negro Improvement Association, had amazing success during the twenties. What is more, the Afro-centric qualities of Ras's appeal as well as his penchant for violence and his reliance on speech as a tool of organization have clear analogues in Garvey's career. Central to Garvey's message was the notion of race pride and even the idea of an ultimate return to Africa that he hoped to finance with various business ventures. The most famous of these was the Black Star Line, a doomed business venture that involved a fleet of transport ships supported by African Americans. Garvey eventually wound up in jail, convicted of fraud as a result of irregularities in this enterprise.

Prior to this time period, however, Garvey was proclaimed "the First Provisional President of Africa," and in a resolution submitted to the Members of the International Conference on Disarmament, Garvey stated: "There can be no peace among us mortals so long as the strong of humanity oppress the weak, for in due process of time and through evolution the weak will one day turn, even like the worm, and then humanity's hope of peace will be shattered."[24] The exhortation to ultimate violence was not unique to this resolution. In a speech concerning the same conference, Garvey declared, "that is why I pointed out to you that your strongest armament is organization, and not so much big guns and bombshells. Later on we may have to use some of those things."[25] Thus, though Garvey's positions changed dramatically over the twenty years during which he was influential, even allying himself on one occasion with the Ku Klux Klan, at various times he emphasized Afro-centrism as well as violence.

Other characteristics of Garvey and his organization tie him to Ras. Leaders in the Universal Negro Improvement Association often wore military regalia, just as Ras does during the final encounter with the narrator during the riot in Harlem. Finally, Garvey saw himself primarily as a speaker, an "exhorter" of sorts. In the introduction to "The Marcus Garvey and UNIA Papers Project," Robert Hill quotes Garvey: "I am a public lecturer, but I am President General of the Universal Negro Improvement Association. As a public lecturer I endeavour to help to educate the public particularly of the race, as I meet that public"[26] Ras's passionate appeal to the narrator and Tod Clifton is clearly an educational exhortation: "When the black man going to tire of this childish perfidity? He got you so you don't trust your black intelligence? You young, don't play you'self cheap, mahn. Don't deny you'self. It took a billion gallons of black blood to make you." (373). Clearly, Ras has characteristics that allow us to tie him to Garvey.

Ras calls himself the "Exhorter," but after the riot at the end of the novel begins, a resident of Harlem refers to him as "Ras the Destroyer" (541), causing the narrator to proclaim, "Ras the Exhorter become Ras the Destroyer." And though Ras is not the cause of the riot at the end of the novel, he is clearly its most well-known spokesperson, taking the place in many respects of the narrator who has unwittingly played into the hands of the Brotherhood's plan for the riot.[27] Thus, Ellison seems to make it clear that the path from exhortation to destruction is a very short one indeed. Both the narrator and Ras demonstrate this to us. Thus, in the final encounter with Ras, we see embodied all of the absurdity and all of the destructive potential of speech. Carrying a shield with "the skin of some wild animal around his shoulder," Ras is to the narrator the embodiment of an "Abyssinian chieftain." Thus, when the narrator grabs Ras's spear in "a desperate oratorical gesture of disagreement" (558), he is protecting himself. But when he throws the spear into the jaws of Ras, he is silencing the exhorter who has replaced him in doing the Brotherhood's biding. "Use a nigger to catch a nigger," (558) he says with high irony. He will speak no more, for as he tells us, he has no more eloquence. What is more, thanks to his gesture, neither will Ras—at least until the spear that locks his jaws is gone. The transition from speaker to writer is completely embodied before our eyes.

When Plato through the mouth of Phaedrus calls the written word an "image" of the spoken word, he sets forth a view of writing and speaking that would haunt Western thought for centuries. Derrida argues that speech has always been privileged in this view because of the distinction that Plato and others draw between speech and writing: in being an image, writing leaves behind the presence of the speaker.[28] As Socrates says, words sown by the pen cannot defend themselves and cannot teach. Ellison's novel puts forth an entirely different position. As a speaker, the narrator is finally absent from the words he speaks, visible as an image of a man but invisible finally as a voice. Only in writing does the narrator feel that he can begin to do what he ultimately calls at the end of the novel, "speak for you." Ellison's novel is the story of a black man's sincere desire and intense struggle to express himself, first through speech and later through writing. Preceding Derrida's work by some ten years, Ellison's novel anticipates in some respects Derrida's critique of what Derrida calls the "phonocentrism" of Western culture. Still, as always in reading Ellison's work, one is tempted to make the matter more symmetrical than it is: if Ellison's narrator rejects speech as a mode of expression, he is still none too comfortable with writing, nor even with the rejection itself. In similar fashion, Derrida's critique of the position of speech in Western culture is not simply a reversal of the role of writing and speaking. Rather, it suggests that the whole relationship between language and presence, language and truth is much more complicated than we might have thought.[29] Ellison's novel seems to make a similar point when we contextualize the story between the prologue and epilogue, when we place speech into the context of writing. It is this latter point that leaves the questions of leadership, ostensibly one of Ellison's central concerns, unanswered at the end of the novel.

The prologue and epilogue move Ellison's story closer to full definition than the story that they support. Significantly, the prologue begins with the sentence "I am an invisible man" (3). The epilogue ends with a question: "And it is this which frightens me: Who knows but that, on the lower frequencies, I speak for you?" (581). These two statements give us the two poles of the rhetorical world: the speaker (or writer) and the audience, the question of who I am and whether I as speaker or writer can represent you, identify with you as reader or listener. Such is the gamble the speaker takes. Such also is the gamble the writer of novels takes. But only in understanding the narrator's position in the prologue and epilogue can we understand this statement and place the story into the context that they create for it. The narrator speaks to us as one who is between, one who knows not what the next move will be: "Yes, but what *is* the next phase?" (576). That writing and perhaps speaking are a vital part of the struggle to define the next phase is clear from the fact that our narrator is a rabble-rouser who has become a writer, that the narrator is "torturing" himself "to put it down" (579). But how he will continue, whether as writer, speaker, both, or neither, is unclear when the novel ends. Still, perhaps answering the question of how to continue is not important to Ellison; perhaps the important issue is dramatizing for us the inadequacy of language to make the self visible. Ellison seems to imply this position in the prologue with the first speech in the novel.

The first speech in *Invisible Man* is easily overlooked. It is not the speech at the Battle Royal. Rather, it is the sermon on "the blackness of blackness." In the prologue to the novel, the narrator smokes a reefer, thinking that it is a cigarette. As he crawls inside "the black and blue" music of Louis Armstrong, he travels into an underground dimension more surreal than the hole in which he lives. It is here on the lower levels of a place that he compares to Dante's hell that he hears the sermon. Echoing the rhetorical traditions of the black church, those that characterize Homer Barbee's speech as well as many of the narrator's most moving orations, the statements he hears vary from being superficially absurd—*"That blackness is most black"* (9)—to being suggestive of a black man or woman's plight in America—

> *Black will make you . . .*
> *Black*
> *. . . or black will un-make you.* (10)

But it is finally the words of the old woman he encounters in his reefer dream that allow us as readers to grasp the importance of the question that Ellison asks here and refuses to answer. Like Louis Armstrong whose music leads us into this realm, she is a singer, but in many respects she embodies all of black history in the United States. The narrator hears her sing a spiritual on "one level" in his dream, but beneath her *"on a still lower level"* he sees *"a beautiful girl the color of ivory pleading in a voice like my mother's as she stood before a group of slaveowners who bid for her naked body"* (italics in original) (10). This old singer of songs is caught between black and white, loving and hating her master who gave her children, who will not set her free, and loving her children who hate her master. She has poisoned her master—*"I loved him and give him the poison and he withered away like a frost-bit apple"* (italics in original) (11). The one thing she loves more than her master is freedom. When the narrator asks her what freedom is, she finally defines it as *"I guess now it ain't nothing but knowing how to say what I got up in my head"* (italics in original) (11). That she cannot find the right words to express herself, that she cannot free herself through language is embodied in her final words to the narrator: *"Leave me 'lone, boy; my head aches!"* (11). As she says earlier, *"Too much done happen to me in too short a time"* (italics in original) (11).

This nightmare vision ultimately defines the dilemma of the black man or woman: one who is caught with more to say than words can express, than language can accommodate, than even "the magic of words" can get across to a reader or listener. Only in the context of a novel that questions the whole nature of language can such a statement be dramatically realized, and only in the context of the desperate need of a black man to express the self can such a statement attain the importance it deserves. The vacuum of leadership that Ellison confronts in this novel renders this whole situation even more dramatic: there is no language for the true horror of African-American experience.[30] Thus, we are left holding the question, "How is a leader to proceed?" As the narrator observes, he shares with his audience "a common dispossession" (345). Only by speaking or writing or in some way communicating this "dispossession" can the novel accomplish its purpose of turning the invisible into the visible. But Ellison seems to imply almost in spite of himself that such might not be possible.

Thus, there are multiple types of invisibility in *Invisible Man*. First there is the invisibility of the black world to the white world. Mr. Norton cannot see the narrator for who he is. Early in the novel, he calls the narrator his destiny. But in the epilogue when the narrator confronts Mr. Norton, saying "But I'm your destiny," the old man stares back as if the narrator were mad. But this invisibility of the black world to the white world is complicated by the invisibility of the self. *"Knowing how to say what I got up in my head"* is the freedom of definition, the ability to be present and to speak the truth, to be the I who is invisible in the prologue and speaks for and to the you who is invisible at the end of the epilogue. Only through becoming visible to "you" does the "I" succeed as a writer, and Ellison's writer begins and ends with the assumption of invisibility. Ellison's novel on its most basic level then is an attempt to speak to you, to overcome invisibility, to state the self, to define being, a black (*"most black"* as the minister says) being that has been squelched, raped, sold, lynched, a black being that hates and loves at once. But in many respects the novel fails in this regard. When all is said and written, the narrator remains an invisible man who speaks for the unknowable, raceless, genderless self that I have argued is, "on the lower frequencies," each one of us. But by creating a self who must speak because of the horror of African-American experience, Ellison succeeds in making us truly grasp what might be the most salient quality of this raceless self: the pain of a language that cannot ever fully live up to its expectation and allow us to speak to or for each other.

Invisible Man is thus a cry from a human voice that never becomes fully visible. It is, as Kristeva argues, a novel about a man in a liminal state who will forever remain on some level invisible.[31] His speeches are finally a sham, but his novel (or "memoirs" as Ellison calls them) allows us at least to glimpse the invisible. But in being a cry, this novel speaks for all of us who must use a language that, as Toni Morrison says in her Nobel Prize acceptance speech, can never really "live up to life itself."[32] In this sense it becomes the divine cry of a human voice, an I that is "most black" and yet tries to define his being through the torturous process of putting words down in black and white for the colorless you who reads the book.

In being a cry, the novel ends in dissonance and uncertainty like the jazz it is so often compared to. What is more, such an ending leaves the critic and the reader with a rather thorny dilemma, for it seems in some respects to put the novel at odds with Ellison's own statements about his work. As quoted above, Ellison said, "The epilogue was necessary to complete the action begun when he [the narrator] set out to write his memoirs." He implies here an action he defines in other places as leaving the underground. But as we noted earlier, the narrator never does so.

This problem is compounded by what has generally been a negative critical reaction to the epilogue. If Ellison intended for the epilogue to "complete the action," as he stated, for many critics his task was unsuccessful. If he sketches here a path out of the underground, for many readers the way out has never been clear. Barbara Foley points out at the opening of her article "The Rhetoric of Anticommunism in *Invisible Man*" that Ellison's epilogue has "routinely evinced dissatisfaction." She then divides critics of the epilogue into three groupings: those who complain about the merging of the author and the narrator, those who complain about the "unproblematic celebration of American democracy," and those who see in the ending a kind of "universalism" that shifts the focus of the novel away from the black condition to the larger issue of the human condition.[33] There are admittedly important critics who find symmetry in Ellison's epilogue, most notably Edith Schor who describes the narrator's "ultimate understanding of his identity as a link in the chain of tradition, [making him] . . . a member of the collectivity, and . . . an individual."[34] Robert Stepto also argues that the epilogue enables the narrator to come to an understanding of his experience, that in becoming a writer he exerts a measure of control over his experience.[35] Still, nowhere does Ellison suggest what role the narrator will play when he gets out of the underground. Thus, despite Ellison's certainty that his character will emerge, the reader is left with a man who still claims to be intrigued by the chaos of the underground, who is still unable to define himself or to become visible.

Readers cannot miss the ambivalence of statements such as these from the last page of the book: "And there's still a conflict within me: With Louis Armstrong one half of me says, 'Open the window and let the foul air out,' while the other says, 'It was good green corn before the harvest,' Of course Louis was kidding, he wouldn't have thrown old Bad Air out, because it would have broken up the music and the dance" (581). Later on the same page the narrator contends, "there's a *possibility* that even an invisible man has a socially responsible role to play" (italics mine) (581). Still later, the narrator contends that the reader's alleged explanation of his motivation—"He only wanted us to listen to him rave!" is "only *partially* true" (italics mine) (581). What emerges from these statements is a man who remains in an unresolved "liminal state," a man who is on the way to transforming himself into some state of which the reader is left no real conception. Indeed, even if we assume, as this chapter has argued, that the novel itself is the fruit of the underground, its focal point is the past. In the present tense of the ending we are still left with a main character intrigued by chaos who seems at least in part to want to stay in the nether light of the underground. What is more, the audience he committed himself to is left without a leader.

Earlier I quoted Ellison's contention that he wrote *Invisible Man* out of "concern with the nature of leadership" among the black community. Such a statement leads one to interesting conclusions, considering the reading of the ending of the novel that I have sketched out here. Not only does the narrator hint at "a socially responsible role" that we never see him assume but also *Invisible Man* was published in 1952, three short years before Rosa Parks refused to relinquish her seat on a Montgomery bus, the first important political confrontation of the Civil Rights movement. That movement brought into being the most important black political leader the country has seen, a man who would clearly be much, much more than the "new Booker T. Washington," as Brother Jack says of the narrator. It is hard not to notice the contrast between the invisible narrator's inarticulate cry and the very visible, articulate fight that Martin Luther King, Jr., led and eventually died for. Moreover, King's great strength was the spoken word, the very medium the narrator of *Invisible Man* seems to reject.

It is high irony indeed that Ellison's novel should begin with a concern for black leadership, posit a protagonist who is poised to emerge from the underground into what might be a socially responsible role four years before Dr. Martin Luther King, Jr., became visible. This irony becomes perplexing when we note Ellison's own response to the movement. Jerry Watts summarizes Ellison's connection (or lack thereof) to the movement quite well in this comment:

> During the past twenty (and perhaps thirty) years, Ellison has not publicly been part of any organized black intellectual effort to confront racist practices in American intellectual life. Other black intellectuals have asked him to use his enormous prestige in this effort, but to no avail.[36]

If we consider active involvement in politics to be synonymous with visibility or emerging from the underground, then we must assume that Ellison, like his narrator, never becomes fully visible.

Though Ellison's reticence on politics has been an issue of contention throughout his career and I run the risk of simplifying it here, the stance takes on new import when we tie it to the ambiguous ending of *Invisible Man* I have proposed here. Who is this man who will "speak for you"? What will his speech be—the novel we have just read, "rabble rousing" that is to come, or the public words of a public man of letters? We are left to wonder. In similar fashion, we were left to wonder about Ellison's long-awaited second novel, the one that never came until John Callahan published a posthumous volume in 1999. If Ellison's invisible man is a black man who cannot be seen by whites as well as the inarticulate self that is each of us, he may also be the man who "raves" behind the mask, the writer behind the well-crafted persona. Could the inarticulate cry of the narrator reflect on some level Ellison's own inability to continue, to lead his persona out of the underground, *"to say what I got in my head"* in the words of the old black woman at the end of the novel"? The long wait for his second novel certainly may suggest such.

Understanding the connection between Ellison and his narrator might allow us to descend into the underground down to the final level of invisibility. But if it is possible at all, it is beyond the scope of this chapter, involving by necessity the more comprehensive examination of the man and his other work that follows. Suffice it here to say that Ellison's concern with language and its limits did not end with *Invisible Man*. Both Alonzo Hickman ("God's Trombone") and Sunraider (or Bliss) from *Juneteenth* are, like the narrator of *Invisible Man*, professional speakers who find themselves left in the end unable to communicate fully as the Senator slowly slips away, hearing the "consoling" voice of Hickman calling to him. And it is perhaps Hickman who provides us with the best assessment of the narrator of *Invisible Man*'s long journey when he tells Bliss of his own preaching on liberation day, Juneteenth: "I had to reach the Word within the Word that was both song and scream and whisper. The Word that was way beyond sense but leaping like a tree of flittering birds with its *own* dictionary of light and meaning."[37] Such a word, we might imagine, is way beyond the surface, somewhere waiting for us in the dark light of the underground

Like Ellison perhaps we all seek that ultimate Word. And like Ellison, perhaps we all fail to find it. But unlike Ellison, few of us, I think, fail with such amazing eloquence.

Notes

1. Robert Stepto has explored this issue carefully in "Literacy and Hibernation in Ralph Ellison's *Invisible Man*." There is, however, an important difference in his explanation of the transformation and mine. He assumes that writing allows the narrator to become "a survivor and a kinsman." I believe that this transformation is not nearly so complete or so tidy. It seems to me that the narrator is still in a state of flux at the end of the novel, a condition that finally reflects Ellison's own ambivalence about his role as a writer.

Robert Stepto, "Literacy and Hibernation in Ralph Ellison's *Invisible Man*," in *Ralph Ellison: Modern Critical Views*, ed. Harold Bloom (New Haven, Conn.: Chelsea House, 1986).

2. Washington records in *Up from Slavery* this surprising response from white America:

I very soon began receiving all kinds of propositions from lecture bureaus, and editors of magazines and papers, to take the lecture platform, and to write articles. One lecture bureau offered me fifty thousand dollars, or two-hundred dollars a night and expenses, if I would place my services at its disposal for a given period.

Booker T. Washington, *Up from Slavery*. In *Three Negro Classics* (New York: Avon, 1965), 150-51.

3. In fact, as late as 1928, a refusal to seek social equality was a quality that black political leaders sometimes used as a way to ingratiate themselves to the white community. Wil Haygood records in *King of the Cats: The Life and Times of Adam Clayton Powell, Jr.* that Oscar DePriest, a black politician elected to

Congress from Chicago, announced publicly, "I have no race consciousness of the kind that is consumed in the vain notions of social equality" (111).

4. Ellison has great fun in this scene with the metafictional aspects of his novel. Booker T. Washington is of course the author of the *Atlanta Exposition Address* that the narrator quotes in his own speech. However, he is also the model for the Founder whom Blind Barbee eulogizes. Thus, when the narrator states that Booker T. was not as great as the Founder, he is contradicting the author. What is more, when the narrator explains himself, the irony deepens: "Well, in the first place, the Founder came before him and did practically everything Booker T. Washington did and a lot more. And more people believed in him. You hear a lot of arguments about Booker T. Washington, but few would argue about the Founder" (306). Jack responds by stating, "No, but perhaps that is because the Founder lies outside of history, while Washington is still a living force" (306).

5. For a good discussion of the ways in which Washington's rhetoric permeates the early chapters of Ellison's novel, see Singleton's previously mentioned essay: "Leadership Mirages as antagonists in *Invisible Man.*"

6. Dolan Hubbard, *The Sermon and the African-American Literary Imagination* (Columbia: University of Missouri Press, 1994), 24.

7. The full quotation here is quite instructive. Though the line quoted above refers to Ellison's work on the famous story "Flying Home" and specifically to the question of African Americans being refused the right to fly planes in combat, the full quotation has a much broader application. "This quarrel led to my concern with the nature of Negro leadership, from a different and nonliterary direction. I was very much involved with the questions of just why our Negro leadership was never able to enforce its will. Just what was there about the structure of American society that prevented Negroes from throwing up effective leaders? Thus it was no accident that the young man in my book turned out to be hungry and thirsty to prove to himself that he could be an effective leader."

Ralph Ellison, "On Initiation Rites and Power," in *The Collected Essays of Ralph Ellison.* ed. John Callahan (New York: Modern Library, 1995) 524-25.

8. Lawrence Jackson, *Ralph Ellison: Emergence of Genius* (New York: John Wiley and Sons, 2001), 311. In fact, his stated "plan of work" in that application came hauntingly close to his actual career. First, he would write a novel on Tuskegee-trained airmen. This project became the story "Flying Home." Then he would write a book on black leadership. The fruit of this project was *Invisible Man.* Then there would be what Jackson calls "a book of criticism" or, quoting Ellison, "'studies in [the] esthetics of Negro forms'" and a collection of stories. Though *Juneteenth* is left off this list and the short stories were not collected until after his death, clearly *Invisible Man, Shadow and Act,* and *Going to the Territory* were in his mind from the start

9. Brian Urquhart. *Ralph Bunche: An American Life* (New York: Norton, 1993), 59.

10. Wil Haygood, *King of the Cats: The Life and Times of Adam Clayton Powell, Jr.* (Boston: Houghton Mifflin, 1993), 112.

11. Ibid., 157.

12. Ibid., 128.

13. Ibid., 146.

14. I should note at this point that Robert Stepto ("Literacy and Hibernation: Ralph Ellison's *Invisible Man*") comes to very different conclusions concerning the narrator's relationship to the Douglass portrait. He argues that in the initial confrontation with the portrait, the narrator fails to grasp or fully understand Douglass's significance or the manner in which he uses writing. He only understands these things later when he goes underground to write and can "*return Douglass's gaze*" (71).

15. Patricia Liggins Hill and Bernard Bell, *Call and Response: The Riverside Anthology of the African-American Literary Tradition* (Boston: Houghton Mifflin, 1998), 272.

16. Ibid., 659.

17. Yonka Kristeva, "Chaos and Pattern in Ellison's *Invisible Man,*" *Southern Literary Journal* 30, no. 4 (1997): 68.

18. Frederick Douglass also addressed women's rights late in his career.

19. Characteristically, Ellison has great fun with puns in the text. The character Tobitt clearly enjoys putting in his "two bits" on every subject, especially the narrator's arranging of a public funeral for Tod Clifton, a man whom the Brotherhood considers a traitor (chapter 22). His pretense of expertise in regard to African Americans is further enhanced by his being married to a black woman. The narrator's assessment of Tobitt's knowledge clearly shows that he considers these connections not to be worth "two bits." The narrator declares sarcastically, "You have our number. In fact, you must be practically a Negro yourself. Was it by immersion or injection?" (468).

20. The reader might also note the moment in the text when the narrator discovers the mechanism by which the Sambo doll works: "Then I saw a fine black thread and pulled it from the frilled paper. There was a loop tied in the end. I slipped it over my finger and stood stretching it taut. And this time it danced." As "Sambo" is controlled by his operators, so the narrator is controlled by the Brotherhood. He sticks to the text that they provide.

21. Plato, *Phaedrus*, in *Readings in Classical Rhetoric*, ed. Thomas W. Benson and Michael H. Prosser, trans. H. N. Fowler (Davis, Calif.: Hermagoras Press, 1988), 39.

22. Ellison, "On Initiation Rites and Power," *TCERE*, 525.

23. Hill, *Call and Response,* 830.

24. Hill, *Call and Response,* 837.

25. Hill, *Call and Response,* 835.

26. Robert Hill, "American Series Introduction," in Garvey and UNIA Papers Project, African Studies Center, UCLA [16]. Available from www.isop.ucla.edu/mgpp/intro01.htm. (April 10, 2003).

27. The narrator's thoughts on this matter are as follows: "I could see it now, see it clearly and in growing magnitude. It was not suicide, but murder. The committee had planned. And I had helped, had been a tool. A tool just at the very moment I had thought myself free" (553).

28. Jacques Derrida, *Of Grammatology* (Baltimore: Johns Hopkins University Press, 1976), 25.

29. Ibid., 56.

30. In a book entitled *Heroism and the Black Intellectual* (Chapel Hill: University of North Carolina Press, 1994) Jerry Gafio Watts, argues that Ellison uses his art as a way of excusing himself from the hard task of the protest and work that brings leadership to African-American issues. Clearly such a position would put an entirely different slant on Ellison's confrontation in this novel of the issue of leadership in African-American affairs. The problem of language could be a way of avoiding the wider problem of culture.

31. Robert B. Stepto also makes this point in the article mentioned in note 2.

32. Toni Morrison, *The Novel Lecture in Literature, 1993* (New York: Knopf, 1994), 21.

33. Barbara Foley, "The Rhetoric of Anticommunism in *Invisible Man*," *College English*, 59 (1997): 530-47.

34. Edith Schor, *Visible Ellison: A Study of Ralph Ellison's Fiction* (Westport, Conn.: Greenwood, 1993), 59. Other critics have also come to similar conclusions. Mark Busby says of the epilogue: "As the narrator prepares for his rebirth, he affirms again part of the Adamic myth of America, thereby becoming an integrative figure, one who contain and consolidates opposing forces."

Mark Busby, *Ralph Ellison* (New York: Twayne, 1991), 59.

35. Stepto, "Literacy and Hibernation," 57.

36. Watts, *Heroism and the Black Intellectual*, 111.

37. Ralph Ellison, *Juneteenth* (New York: Vintage, 1999), 139.

Chapter Three

A Socially Responsible Role for an Invisible Man: Ellison the Essayist

"Life for the novelist is a game of hide and seek in which he is eternally the
sometimes delighted but more often frustrated 'it.'"
—Ralph Ellison, "Society, Morality, and the Novel"

Ralph Ellison ended his remarks at the funeral of his friend Romare
Bearden by saying that "Art is the mystery that gets left out of history."[1]
Some twenty-four years earlier, Ellison ended his famous essay "The
World and the Jug" by drawing a similar connection between politics and
novel writing. Directly addressing his antagonist Irving Howe ("Dear
Irving, I am still yakking on"), Ellison insists, "I am enlisted for the duration [in the "Negro Freedom Movement"]." He then observes, "no Negroes are beating down my door," noting that "my Negro friends recognize a certain division of labor among the members of the tribe. Their
demands, like that of many whites, are that I publish more novels." [2]
Ellison insists here that his role in what he calls the "Negro Freedom
Movement" is that of novel writing. Both of these statements give to the
artist a rather important position—one somewhere between activist by
default and interpreter of events that do not register on the historical ra-
dar screen. Furthermore, the latter statement from "The World and the
Jug" implies that novelists might consider themselves to be political by

virtue of writing novels, regardless of other activities in which they might or might not choose to participate.[3]

Ironically, a few short years after Ellison's pointed reply to Irving Howe in "The World and the Jug," other members of "his tribe" were doing more than beating down his door; they were actively heckling him when he spoke and openly calling him an "Uncle Tom."[4] Clearly, these fellow African Americans did not read Ellison's novel or essays as important political or historical proclamations—they read them as accommodation to a status quo that had too long controlled African-American understanding of the self. Ellison, however, apparently continued to think of himself as fulfilling an important role in American culture by writing novels, by being a public man of letters, for he persisted in his task. And though he did on occasion accuse himself of being remiss in not finishing his second novel,[5] he worked toward that end until he died at eighty with the second novel still incomplete. All the while, he continued to write essays that examined the role of literature and art in culture and in particular the role of the novel in American culture. Though examining these writings cannot settle the dispute that continues to swirl around Ellison's work because of what many perceive as its political reticence, such an examination can move us in the direction of understanding the role that Ellison thought the novel and the novelist should play in American culture. Such as examination can also help us to understand the complications faced by that invisible man Ellison left at the end of *Invisible Man* poised to come out of the underground to take on a "socially responsible role." As I argued in the previous chapter, that invisible man has much in common with Ellison himself.

More than any other novelist in American history with the exception of Henry James or perhaps William Dean Howells, Ellison attempted to explain the art of the novel and thereby to locate himself as a novelist in what he considered to be the tradition of the American novel.[6] In *Ralph Ellison: Emergence of Genius*, Lawrence Jackson shows clearly that Ellison was an established critic before he was a novelist. In fact, prior to publishing *Invisible Man*, Ellison's reputation rested primarily on his having been editor of *Negro Quarterly* and two remarkable review essays that appeared in the mid-forties: "Richard Wright's Blues" in the summer 1945 issue of the *Antioch Review* and "Beating that Boy" in the October 22, 1945, issue of the *New Republic*.[7] Though Ellison always spoke of himself as a novelist and not as a critic or even an essayist, the quality of his essays suggests that they were more than momentary preoccupations. He gave them quite literally his full attention.[8] Presumably, that is why they continue to be regarded highly by those inside and outside of the academy. But can they help us to discover a rationale for the novel as a part of politics and history? Can they shed light on what was happening while Ellison wrote these essays: the construction of the long-awaited second novel? Do the essays shed light on that process and possibly explain why it was never completed? Though the latter is likely a question that can never be fully answered, exploring the essays is worth the effort if such an exploration moves us to a better understanding of Ellison the novelist. Furthermore, since Ellison completed only one novel in his lifetime and two collections of essays, we must assume that whatever else they may tell us, the essays form a vital part of the literary career of Ralph Ellison, so much so that without examining them one cannot hope to understand Ellison.

In one of his many essays on jazz, Ellison described the word "Bop" thus: "A word which throws up its hands in clownish self-deprecation before all the complexity of sound and rhythm and self-assertive passion which it pretends to name."[9] One might make a similar observation about the novel. Forced to find a single critical concept that will explain the sheer lunacy of Melville's *Moby Dick*, the adolescent self-absorption of Salinger's *The Catcher in the Rye*, and the multilayered, time-jumbled narrative structure of Faulkner's *Absalom, Absalom!,* a critic can hardly be blamed for failing to be tidy. The best critic might be justified in choosing a term that is in essence a "throwing up of the hands." The definitions of the novel that we will examine here and use as a foundation for our discussion of Ellison's concepts are essentially that.

Mikhail Bakhtin in his essay "Epic and Novel" speaks of the novel as "plasticity itself," insisting that "the utter inadequacy of literary theory is exposed when it is forced to deal with the novel."[10] Both Northrop Frye and Richard Chase tend to define the novel by saying what it is not. It is not in the true sense of the term the romance, but it does have some connection to the romance, so much so that a pure novel might not exist. And yet a novel that is pure romance is not a novel at all. Frye observes, "Pure examples of either form [novel or romance] are never found; there is hardly any modern romance that could not be made out to be a novel, and vice versa."[11] Richard Chase in *The American Novel and Its Tradition* says of romance and novel that "these terms have to be defined closely enough to distinguish between them, even though the distinction itself may sometimes be meaningless as applied to a given book."[12] Chase then makes the distinction that we find often in attempts to separate novel from romance. The novel is close and "comprehensive" in its adherence to reality whereas the romance "renders reality in less volume and detail."[13] But using Henry James's theories of the novel, Chase finds more romance than reality in the American novel. In this regard we might remember Hawthorne (a writer whom Chase pays great homage to just as Henry James and Ralph Ellison did) who had a habit of calling all of his novels romances in his self-effacing prefaces to them and chastising himself for being nothing but a writer of romances. Despite these caveats, critics have persisted in calling him a novelist and ranking him among the best.

Thus, we might conclude that the novel is a fluid genre and that a completely satisfying definition will never be fashioned. Perhaps Emory Elliott posits the safest approach to defining the novel when in *The Columbia History of the American Novel* he defines the novel as "a text of substantial length that is normally written in prose and presents a narrative of events involving experiences of characters who are representative of human agents."[14] He then adds, "This definition probably does not account for every text now accepted as a novel—and will account for fewer with the appearance of every new experimental work."[15] Elliott's definition is safe, but it is so broad that it is of limited use to that person who would understand the politics of a particular novelist. For us it merely underscores the open-ended nature of the form, reminding us that it may be futile to define a form that so rapidly transforms itself that it defies definition.

Bakhtin says at another point in his essay, that the novel is "anticanonical,"[16] implying that the novel redefines itself every generation or so, perhaps every time a serious writer attempts to write a serious novel. At another point in the essay, Bakhtin describes the novel's tendency to parody itself.[17] Cleary cognizant of these qualities of the novel, Ellison writes in "Hidden Name and Complex Fate" that "the writer's greatest freedom" is technique. Thereby, the writer finds "the freedom to possess and express the meaning of his life."[18] Similarly, at the end of his acceptance speech for the 1952 National Book Award, Ellison uses the image of Proteus to describe the novel.[19] Since Proteus was by definition a formless being who could assume whatever shape benefited him most, Ellison seems to agree with Bakhtin that the novel is "plasticity itself." But far from being an impediment, Ellison, like Bakhtin, sees this "plasticity" as liberating. We might also remember two additional points in relation to Ellison's statement. First, the Proteus of Greek mythology was not only formless but also prophetic. Second, this formlessness of the novel is very much like the formlessness of jazz: a quality that encourages the artist to experiment and to define the artistic self in very individualistic form.

Still, despite the plasticity of novel form and the liberation that promises to the serious novelist, there are certain salient characteristics that do tend to tie novelists together. Thus, though we may not be able to define the novel or force it into one shape or another, we can identify certain motivations that most novelists seem to share. The most important of these characteristics is contemporaneity. In large measure novels are not concerned with what happened years and years ago; rather, they are concerned with what happens now. And though there are certainly novelists who write about the past, they often seem to do so with an eye to the present. Thus, though Hawthorne's *The Scarlet Letter* may be set in the Puritan past, it is very much a picture of reality that radically questions the unrestrained optimism of the Transcendentalist movement in mid-nineteenth-century America. And though Sir Walter Scott's novels are nostalgic tales of medieval England, they celebrate a kind of heroism that questions the values of industrialized England. Thus, recalling Frye's statement that there are no pure novels or romances or Chase's argument that the American novel contains a large measure of romance, we can conclude that to the degree that a novel is a novel at all, it will be concerned in some way with the present. And though Hawthorne and Scott may be writing romances, they are romances that betray a desire on the part of their authors to question the reality of the present. To this degree they are novels.

A second quality that all novelists share is a concern with the individual and the individual's relationship to the world around him or her, in particular the world of society. In his *Anatomy of Criticism* Frye borrows from Aristotle's *Poetics* five levels of mimesis. According to Frye, each of these levels is grounded upon a particular relationship between the hero and the world around the hero. The world in this regard consists of other human beings and the environment. If the hero is "superior in kind" to both of these, the story is a myth. If the hero is superior in degree to both, the story is a romance. If the hero is superior in degree to other men but not to his environment, then the work in question is a tragedy or an epic. The last two categories fall into what Frye calls the "low mimetic" and the "ironic mode." In the first of these the hero is superior neither to others nor to his or her environment. He or she is, in Frye's phrase, "one of us."[20] In the ironic mode, the hero is inferior to the reader or observer, who is "looking down on a scene of bondage, frustration or absurdity."[21] Including in his sweeping view of fiction the last fifteen centuries of

Western literature, Frye argues that writers have consistently moved
down the list of categories, so that modern literature deals primarily in
the low mimetic or the ironic mode. Appearing in the late seventeenth
and early eighteenth centuries, the novel falls into one of the latter two
categories. The novel is always concerned with what Frye calls "one of
us" or what we might term one below us. ("Who knows but that, on the
lower frequencies, I speak for you?" writes Ellison's Invisible Man
[581].) Rarely, it would seem, does the novel go beyond the realm of the
average human being faced with the problems of society and the environment that average human beings face.

Similar to Frye, Bakhtin also argues that the novel is concerned with
man and woman as one of us, stating that the novel is the only form of
literature that can explore human beings in their dynamic positions as
members of society. The novel is thus "dialogic." In one sense this
means that the novel is always an artistic utterance that is evoked by
other artistic utterances and thereby evokes other utterances—hence the
anticanonical quality of the novel that we discussed earlier. Novelists are
constantly re-creating the form and parodying earlier novels. But in addition to this social quality of the novel, Bakhtin sees the novel as being
internally dialogic. The systems of language and the people within novels are ultimately ideological in that they express the position of groups
within society rather than simply individuals. Bakhtin writes, "every language in the novel is a point of view, a socio-ideological conceptual system of real social groups and their embodied system."[22] Thus, according
to Bakhtin, the novel has the capacity to mirror the complexity of life, to
put man and woman into motion as a dynamic, social being. The end result is a work where motion does not end. According to Bakhtin, with the
novel as with life there is no "final word."[23]

The contemporaneity of the novel as well as its concern with man and
woman in the midst of their fellow beings is predicated upon what may
be the single most important quality of the novel, namely, its ability to
reflect reality. Ian Watt's work in the theory of the novel deals with this
issue probably better than any other novel theorist. Watt distinguishes
among the mid-nineteenth-century movement called realism, the concept
of philosophical realism brought into being with Descartes and Locke,
scholastic realism of the Middle Ages, and the realism of the novel.[24] In
making these distinctions, he gives us a very thorough understanding of
the way in which the novel differs from other forms of literature. According to Watt the novel reflects the modern concern with the particu-
lars of individual experience as opposed to the premodern concern with

the group experience and the type. Thus, Watt sees as central in the formation of the novel the very qualities that Ellison returns to again and again in his assessment of the novel form: contemporary reality and individuality. Thus, the novel becomes the literary genre that is most able to convey the individual's struggle in the context of society. What is more, given the plasticity of the novel's form, it is the only genre capable of adapting itself to the individual utterance in the context of a society that is in a constant state of flux

That Ellison's idea of the novel should accord with the defining qualities of the novel that I have set forth above should surprise no one. Ellison clearly saw himself as a part of the broad tradition of the American novel, a tradition that grows out of the European novel.[25] His essays are filled with statements concerning the novel that put at the forefront of the art form those very concerns that we have just discussed: contemporaneity, society and the individual, and the everyday reality of the individual American life. In fact, the basic definition of the novel that Ellison gives us in his 1957 essay, "Society, Morality, and the Novel," touches each one of these points rather handily:

> I believe that the primary social function of the novel (the function from which it takes its form and which brought it into being) is that of seizing from the flux and flow of our daily lives those abiding patterns of experience which, through their repetition and consequences in our affairs help to form our sense of reality, and from which emerge our sense of humanity and our conception of human value.[26]

What is more interesting perhaps is the one quality that Ellison adds to this rather traditional definition: human value. In essence, Ellison is adding to his rather traditional definition of the novel the concept of the novel as a moral act.[27] We do not have to argue that novels and morality never go together in the history of American novels in order to notice the pronounced emphasis that Ellison gives to this feature of the novel, nor do we have to accept at face value Faulkner's famous lines to Jean Stein in 1956: "He [the writer] is completely amoral in that he will rob, borrow, beg, or steal from anybody and everybody to get the work done."[28] Ellison was not the first or the only novelist to see moral concerns as central in his conception of the novel. Notwithstanding his well-known statement, Faulkner would have doubtlessly agreed. Nonetheless, Ellison seems to place unusual emphasis upon the moral concerns of the novelist, perhaps more than any other major American novelist. This is not a concern that appears only in the title and content of the 1957 "Society,

Morality, and the Novelist," an essay we will examine in more detail later, but also one that appears in the earliest of Ellison's critical essays.

Even in "Twentieth Century Fiction and the Black Mask of Humanity," an essay written in 1946, six years before *Invisible Man* was published, Ellison insists upon the basic moral responsibility of the novelist. Distinguishing between the European and the American novel, Ellison indicts the American novel for its reticence on moral issues:

> In the United States, as in Europe, the triumph of industrialism has repelled the artist with the blatant hypocrisy between its ideals and its acts. But while in Europe the writer became the most profound critic of these matters, in our country he either turned away or was at best half-hearted in his opposition. [29]

Ellison speculates that the reason for the American writer's reticence on these matters is race. The American writer cannot confront the basic moral contradictions of the culture because the most basic of these is the unfulfilled promise of the Declaration of Independence and the Constitution to create a system in which all men are treated equally. This idea, which would be seminal in *Invisible Man* and *Juneteenth*, appears in Ellison's writing as early as 1941. In a draft version of an essay named "Richard Wright and Negro Fiction" that would later appear in *Direction* in 1941, Ellison writes, "The future of democracy is seen as wraped [sic] up in the development of the Negro."[30] Though this statement is edited out of the published draft of the essay, it clearly demonstrates the consistency with which Ellison connected morality to the novel and the novel to democracy.

Ellison sounds the morality theme seven years later in 1953 in the speech that he gave accepting the National Book Award for *Invisible Man*. And though this time he does not initially tie the issue to race, he once again sees morality as the responsibility of the novelist. He opens his speech by posing a hypothetical question concerning "the chief significance" of *Invisible Man,* his "not quite fully achieved attempt at a major novel." Ellison states that his novel is significant for two reasons—its experimental attitude and "its attempt to return to the mood of personal moral responsibility for democracy which typified the best of our nineteenth-century fiction."[31] Later in the speech, Ellison specifically identifies two American writers who fulfill what he sees as the novelist's moral responsibility. The nineteenth-century tradition of moral responsibility ended with Mark Twain, and of twentieth-century authors, only William Faulkner has carried the burden. At this point in the speech, he links moral responsibility to race consciousness: "their works [those of nineteenth-century American writers] were imaginative projections of the conflicts within the human heart which arose when the sacred principles of the Constitution and the Bill of Rights clashed with the practical exigencies of human greed and fear, hate and love."[32] He later clarifies his reference here by stating that in these writers "the Negro was the gauge of the human condition as it waxed and waned in our democracy."[33] As in the 1946 essay, Ellison links America's moral condition to the treatment of what he calls the "Negro," but unlike his position in that essay, he argues that in the case of nineteenth-century American writers and Faulkner, American writers do indeed confront the problem.

At this point in his National Book Award speech, Ellison brings into his argument the image of Proteus mentioned above, but in so doing, he makes another connection that we do not find in most theories of the novel. He implies that only through linking moral responsibility with an experimental attitude can the novelist come up to the standards of the past: "What has been missing from so much experimental writing has been the passionate will to dominate reality as well as the laws of art."[34] Expanding upon this point, Ellison states that Proteus is not simply a model for the experimental nature of novel form. According to Ellison, "Proteus stands for both America and the inheritance of illusion through which all men must fight to achieve reality; the offended god stands for our sins against those principles we all hold sacred."[35] He ends his speech by stating that Americans always return to "fundamentals" in times of "crisis" and that in *Invisible Man* he as a writer has done just that.

The idea of "crisis" is one we cannot pass over without comment. What, one may ask, was the crisis that America confronted in the late forties and early fifties when Ellison wrote and published *Invisible Man*? In one sense the word "crisis" refers to the state of the novel. Early in the speech Ellison states, "there is a crisis in the American novel."[36] This is also a concern that he returns to in "Society, Morality and the Novel" four years later. But Ellison makes it very clear that his use of the term crisis is tied not just to form but also to content and its relation to American life: "The explosive nature of events mocks our brightest efforts," he states.[37] Though somewhat less venomous, this statement echoes again the indictment of the American novel that we find in the 1946 essay "Twentieth Century Fiction and the Black Mask of Humanity." Ellison suggests that American writers as a whole do not confront the true issues of American life. "The prestige of the theorists of the so-called novel of manners has been challenged,"[38] he states at another point in the speech. Thus, illusion or turning of the head is the center of the crisis in American fiction. His return to "fundamentals" then is an attempt to face the "crisis," not by looking at manners but by looking at the reality beneath them: "Our task then is always to challenge the apparent forms of reality—that is, the fixed manners and values of the few."[39] Therefore, the crisis in the novel reflects the inability of Americans to face the harsh reality of the inequities of American life, a crisis in art that reflects a crisis in American identity.

Placing these words in their historical context clarifies to some extent Ellison's view of the role of the novelist. Most Americans would have felt prosperous and peaceful during this time period. It is hard to imagine a time when the notion of national crisis would have been less likely to be on the national agenda, especially given the fact that the first half of the decade of the 1940s was one of war and the decade preceding the forties was one of depression. The only crisis most Americans would have been aware of was the Cold War, a situation that by its very name was not a crisis in an ongoing sense of the term. And though the stakes in the Cold War might have been very high indeed, the reality of imminent destruction was only occasionally front-page news in incidents such as the Cuban Missile Crisis in the early 1960s. Given the fact that Ellison does not mention the powers involved in the Cold War and does mention "our sins against those principles that we hold sacred," he seems clearly to insist that the state of civil rights is the central crisis in American life. And though most Americans would have considered the problem to be one that hovered in the background of a burgeoning, rampant American prosperity or even an impending World War III, Ellison insists in this speech that it be an issue in the foreground.

If we return to Ellison's image of "fighting" with Proteus, a clearer picture begins to emerge of just the role that Ellison envisioned for his first novel: a wrestling with illusion that most Americans held so that the reality of the crisis becomes apparent through both the form and the content of the novel.[40] And thus, as I have argued in chapter two, Ellison's invisible narrator is left poised to come out of the underground at this moment of exposing the national crisis. He has undergone the transformation that wrestling with a god brings: he lives in a world of light, and though this world is underground and out of sight, he lives on to contemplate a "socially responsible role" for an invisible man.

Still other parts of Ellison's surprising last statement need to be examined if we are to understand fully the role he sets forth for the novelist

here. Ellison states that Americans return to "fundamentals" in times of
crisis and that he has done just that in *Invisible Man*. Is Ellison referring
to fundamentals of the Constitution and the Declaration of Independence,
the fundamentals of the form of the novel, or both? He has mentioned
both throughout the speech. The narrator of Ellison's novel in his final
evaluation of his grandfather's deathbed advice sees the possibility that
after all of the irony and ambiguity that he had imputed to his grandfather's last words, the old man might simply have meant what he said:
"overcome 'em with yeses" (16). "Did he mean to say 'yes' because he
knew that the principle was greater than the men, greater than the numbers and the vicious power and all the methods used to corrupt its
name?" (574) asks Ellison's narrator. Still, in many respects Ellison's
narrator does not envision a world in which these "fundamentals" are
achieved. He only sees the world as it is from his enlightened cave: the
insight comes, but in what way does the narrator discharge his "personal
moral responsibility for democracy"—simply by writing a novel that
questions and destroys for him personally a national illusion? Can the
form of the novel itself be the "fundamental" that Ellison insists Americans return to in times of crisis? If so, given the formlessness we have
found at the center of novel form, what would the fundamental form of
the novel be? Would it be simply the confrontation with the raw facts of
American life that most novelists seem to avoid? Answering these questions drives us back to the image of Proteus at the center of the speech.

The story of wrestling with Proteus, which might apply to both novelist and narrator, does not end with mere insight: it ends with direction.
Addressing all "who struggle with form and with America," Ellison
quotes in his acceptance speech Eidothea's words to Menelaus from the
Odyssey:

> She tells him to seize her father, Proteus, and to hold him fast "however
> he may struggle and fight. He will turn into all sorts of shapes to try
> you," she says, "into all the creatures that live and move upon the earth,
> into water, into blazing fire, but you must hold him fast and press all the
> harder. When he is himself and questions you in the same shape that he
> was when you saw him in his bed, let the old man go; and then, sir, ask
> which god it is who is angry, and how you shall make your way home-
> wards over the fish-giving sea."[41]

As an ultimate description of the novelist, this image accords well
with both the author and the narrator of *Invisible Man*. Ellison the novelist sees wrestling with chaos and illusion and form to be the role of the

novelist. The narrator of *Invisible Man* has wrestled throughout the novel with one illusion after another from his grandfather (who, like Proteus, is constantly changing his form) to the white men at the Battle Royal to Ras the Destroyer. But neither writer nor character seems to accomplish what Eidothea insists that Menelaus achieve: to find the angry god and to head homeward. Nonetheless, in this important speech, Ellison the writer defines that homeward journey in one of his most eloquent statements ever about the nature of democracy: "The way home we seek is that condition of man's being at home in the world, which is called love, and which we term democracy."[42] The idealism of these words puts their reality beyond either the facts of American life or the fictional reality of the narrator of *Invisible Man*, who, like the central character in Richard Wright's "The Man Who Lived Underground," is literally and metaphorically underground, shut off from American society. It is for that reason that Ellison states that we "seek" the way home, rather than that we have found it.

What emerges from this speech is a role for the novelist that staggers the imagination. The novelist must wrestle with reality and provide for his culture a way of overcoming illusion, thereby accepting moral responsibility for democracy, pointing the moral direction for the culture. Such a novelist would indeed be more than the artist who writes for fame or money or even to create beauty or truth or some combination of the two. He or she would be the artist as medicine man, soothsayer, bard, national conscience—the prophetic one who points the culture in the direction in which it must go. And by any measure, a novelist who fulfills the description put forward by Ellison would be political. If the novelist shatters the illusions of those around him and then identifies the angry god while pointing homeward, he or she is indeed the essence of politics.[43] Otherwise, the whole notion of being responsible for democracy has no credibility. If *Invisible Man* is, as Ellison describes it, a "not quite fully achieved attempt at a major novel," then perhaps the vision of the novelist described here suggests a second novel that will truly stagger the imagination. Furthermore, given the fact that Ellison's narrator is living underground at the end of *Invisible Man*, we must assume that he is far from home, that he is still seeking "that condition of man's being at home in the world."[44]

Ellison's concern with morality, democracy, and individualism does not end with the speeches I have covered thus far. It appears in almost every essay he wrote concerning the role of the novelist. Some seven years after the acceptance speech, Ellison sounds a similar theme in "Stephen Crane and the Mainstream of American Fiction," his introduction to a volume of Stephen Crane's writing. Ellison states that in most of Crane's fiction the central point is "the cost of moral perception, of achieving an informed sense of life, in a universe which is essentially hostile to man and in which skill and courage and loyalty are virtues which help in the struggle but by no means exempt us from the necessary plunge into the storm-sea-war of experience."[45] Though it is not clear why Ellison leaves Crane out of what we will call "the moral tradition of the novel" in his 1953 speech and then puts him in seven years later, this introduction underscores again the centrality of a moral vision for the serious novelist and again suggests that moral perception only comes with a struggle, much like the struggle with Proteus that he describes in the National Book Award speech. Indeed, the very use of the word "struggle" recalls the imagery of the 1953 speech.

Still, Ellison's most complete examination of the role of the novelist in American society occurs in the essay with which we started our discussion: "Society, Morality, and the Novel." Written in 1957, a year before the Crane essay and four years after the National Book Award speech, this essay begins with Ellison's characteristic identification of himself as a novelist and not a critic. He writes that theorizing about the novel leads one into the fields of "social and aesthetic criticism," what he calls "systems of thought," whereas the novelist's true role is "to play with the fires of chaos and to rearrange reality to the patterns of his imagination."[46] Every novel, writes Ellison, is "a discussion of craft." [47] Notwithstanding these self-deprecating comments, Ellison examines very carefully the role of the novelist in American culture. And the most important part of what he argues comes first. He states that in the sense that the novel plays upon "our shared assumptions," it is "communication" and thereby it is "rhetorical."[48] To say that the novel is communication is one matter; to say that it is rhetorical is quite another. The word "rhetorical" implies persuasion and thus suggests that the novelist is involved in the enterprise of convincing readers of the validity of his or her point of view.[49] At this point Ellison picks up once again the argument he first forged in the 1946 essay "Twentieth Century Fiction and the Black Mask of Humanity": the notion of the novelist as the one who force feeds reality to those who do their best to evade it. Italicizing his words, Ellison argues that the admiration that a novelist achieves is directly related, *"to the extent that he justifies our desire to evade certain aspects of reality which we find unpleasant beyond the point of confrontation."*[50]

In forcing us to confront the unpleasant face of reality, the novelist *"justifies our desire to evade"*—he or she reminds us of why we would rather not look reality in the eye. The form of this statement is intriguing. *"Justifies"* is an odd choice for a novelist who has consistently argued that Americans are blind to the injustice all around them. But here Ellison almost seems to argue that injustice of this sort is a fact of life, a part of the donnée of any reality one might find. Alluding to the Book of John from the New Testament, Ellison states a few sentences later, "In the beginning was not only the word but the contradiction of the word."[51] Thus, the novelist is forever exposing contradiction to those who would rather look the other way, those who might even be *justified* in looking the other way. And it is this role that underscores what Ellison calls the "usefulness" of the novel, for it thrives on "change and social turbulence."[52] What is more, if the novel did not exist "it would have been necessary for Americans to invent it."[53] Ellison argues that only in the United States are "class lines so fluid and change so swift *and intentional*" (italics in original) as to require constant reevaluation in order to reach a sense of self-definition. Americans are not yet completely conscious of themselves, states Ellison, and the novel must ultimately play a role in American self-definition.[54] There follows a by now familiar indictment of certain American writers—specifically those of the "lost generation" and the rebellious thirties as well as the modern day. In fact, those novelists as well as others in American life have been guilty of "moral evasion." Those who were *not* guilty on this ground are again the core writers of nineteenth-century American literature: Hawthorne, Melville, James, and Twain.

It seems likely that "Society, Morality, and the Novel," constituted an essay that expressed many of Ellison's most carefully worked out ideas of what a novel should be. Among Ellison's papers at the Library of Congress, there are two thick folders of drafts of the essay, many of them heavily marked with revisions. More importantly Ellison had trouble meeting the deadline for the essay imposed by the editor Granville Hicks. Hicks initiated the project in an attempt to produce a book called *The Living Novel* in which practicing novelists discussed the form, and he approached Ellison concerning the project. Ellison readily agreed to write an essay for the book, but he was the last of the contributors to finish his essay. Hicks wrote to him imposing a deadline of April 1, 1957, stating that any manuscript received after that date would not be included in the text. Ellison sent Hicks half of his essay on March 26, 1957, promising to send the rest shortly. He then attempted in his letter to sum up his view of the state of the novel: "Criticism has worked to narrow our conception of the novel and thus for all of its concern with aesthetics it has managed to cut the novel core out of those novels which it recommends. It has thus played a fairly insidious moral role itself."[55] This statement is ironic in view of the self-deprecating statements with which the essay begins. Ellison may indeed feel that a novelist is better off writing novels than writing about novels, but clearly when the novelist begins to consider the work of critics, he recognizes that critics do not understand the central concerns of the novelist. It would almost seem that the novelist is justified in this regard in pausing and explaining himself or herself. Very much like Henry James, Ellison seems to feel more than the need to write novels; he also feels the need to explain how they function.

By now it should be clear that Ellison places at the center of the novelist's concerns the issue of "personal moral responsibility for democracy" and that he finds that many novelists in his culture fall short in this regard. What is more, he sees this responsibility as vital to American consciousness and to the ongoing process of American self-definition. We must now examine this whole notion in relation to Ellison's own comments concerning the political nature of his work. Two of Ellison's most famous essays will concern us here, both from the years 1963 and 1964: "The World and the Jug" and "Unknown Name and Complex Fate." Do these essays in any way change the basic assumptions that we find Ellison making in the essays that he wrote in the forties and fifties or do they merely confirm those assumptions in the context of a rapidly changing culture that was becoming increasingly attuned to the political nature of art? It is this question that will concern the balance of this chapter.

Arguably Ellison's most famous essay, "The World and the Jug" was a response to Irving Howe's "Black Boys and Native Sons," an essay that appeared in the autumn 1963 issue of *Dissent*. Ellison's response was evoked not only by what he considered to be an attack on his work but also more directly by a request from Myron Kolatch of *The New Leader*. As Ellison explains in his introduction to the essay in Callahan's *The Collected Essays of Ralph Ellison*, Kolatch first telephoned for Ellison's response, and then he requested that Ellison put the response in the form of an essay. The response takes place in two parts—first a simple reply and then a reply to Howe's reply, which had appeared in *The New Leader* in February 1964. When "The World and the Jug" appeared in *Shadow and Act* in 1964, both the initial reply and the response to Howe's reply appeared together. The essay is instructive in several ways. First, Ellison's description of the role of the novelist is remarkably consistent with what he says of the novel in the earlier essays that we have discussed. Second, the essay has brought forth a number of responses from Ellison's critics. Finally, Ellison fails to respond to one of Howe's central complaints about *Invisible Man*.

As Ellison himself says in his introductory comments to "The World and the Jug" in *The Collected Essays of Ralph Ellison*, Howe's argument is difficult to summarize in a sentence or two. Readers who really want to understand it should read the essay itself. Nonetheless, a brief summary can identify those portions of the essay that Ellison responds to. Howe basically establishes a dichotomy in the recent history of African-American literature between Richard Wright (a "Native Son") and the two dominant black writers who followed him, James Baldwin and Ralph Ellison ("Black Boys").[56] Howe's ostensible aim in the essay is to answer some of the criticism that Baldwin had leveled against Wright in two well-known essays: "Everybody's Protest Novel" and "Many Thousand Gone." True to that motivation, he uses most of the essay to defend Wright against the attacks of Baldwin. What is more, there is much in the essay that simply establishes Wright's dominance as a writer, in particular as *the* black writer who came first and established the ground upon which later black writers would tread. As Howe states early in the essay, "If such younger novelists as Baldwin and Ralph Ellison were to move beyond Wright's harsh naturalism and toward more supple modes of fiction, that was possible only because Wright had been there first, courageous enough to release the full weight of his anger."[57] Howe's essay is no doubt given special resonance by the fact that Wright was a friend of Howe's and that he had died in 1960, some three years before Howe wrote his essay.

Surprisingly, though Ellison's response would not lead us to think as much, Howe writes the essay primarily about Baldwin and Wright, fully discussing Ellison only late in the essay and then by way of example. Much of what Howe says in the essay is very complimentary of Ellison: "The Negro writer who has come closest to satisfying Baldwin's program is not Baldwin himself but Ralph Ellison, whose novel *Invisible Man* is a brilliant though flawed achievement, standing with *Native Son* as the major fiction thus far by American Negroes."[58] Given the fact that Howe finds large-scale faults in all of Baldwin's novels and with *Native Son* also, it would seem that Ellison fairs rather well in this essay. Nonetheless, when Kolatch asked for a response for *The New Leader*, Ellison composed an excoriating attack upon Howe. One learns a great deal about Ellison's view of his role as novelist by looking at his objections.

One also learns a great deal by looking at those issues that he fails to mention in his response.

The center of Ellison's complaint is that Howe assumes the role of determining what African-American fiction should be and thereby what the African-American experience behind it has been. This is indeed an irony that is hard to miss, for Howe consistently describes African-American experience as if it were his own: "How could a Negro put pen to paper, how could he so much as think or breathe without some impulsion to protest, be it harsh or mild, political or private, released or buried?"[59] One might legitimately wonder how a white man could ask such a question without having lived the experience he is speculating about. And though Howe's intent is clearly to emphasize the enormous role that racial discrimination has played in the lives of black Americans, he relinquishes in the process his critical distance from his subject by claiming an insight that is simply not humanly possible. Such concerns form the center of Ellison's response. Ellison embodies much of his critique in the metaphor that we find in the title of the essay. According to Ellison, Howe assumes that segregated African Americans live in "an opaque steel jug" awaiting a messiah. To Howe, that messiah is Wright. But Ellison states that if segregation does isolate African Americans, it is inside a clear jug, outside of which they can see, read, and form values. The central question is thus one of experience. What is African-American experience and who gets the right to identify and use it?

We began our discussion of Ellison's view of the novel by focusing upon the definition he gives us of the novel in "Society, Morality, and the Novel." According to that definition the novelist seizes "from the flux and flow of our daily lives those abiding patterns of experience which through their repetition and consequences in our affairs help to form our sense of reality, and from which emerge our sense of humanity and our conception of human value."[60] Questioning the novelist's ability to read those experiences rather than his ability to transform them into art suggests an attack not upon art but upon individuality—the individual's ability to know his own life and the life around him or her. Such a critique violates one of the central tenets of Jamesian criticism, the donnée. As James argues in the famous essay "The Art of Fiction," "Of course, it is of execution that we are talking—that being the only point of a novel that is open to contention. This is perhaps too often lost sight of, only to produce great confusion and cross purposes."[61] Thus, according to James, we must grant the artist his subject before we begin to attack what he or she is able to make of that subject. Striking a similar pose, Ellison argues: "What moves a writer to eloquence is less meaningful than what he makes of it."[62] Ellison argues further that in Howe's critique, ideas are being "imposed between me and my sense of reality."[63] This observation leads Ellison to one of the more famous declarations in the essay, one that Howe cites in his response as an example of Ellison's having lost control: "I fear the social order which it [Howe's insistence that black artist express a "clenched militancy"] forecasts more than I do that of Mississippi."[64] In Ellison's response to Howe's response he repeats this statement "coldly," insisting that this is a statement of logic and not one of anger.

The issue at the center of this conflict is the freedom to confront experience, but on a more subtle level it is also the freedom to interpret that experience as a writer. Ellison argues that the only goal that he has sought in his career is the freedom to be called "writer."[65] Moreover, the point he argues has historical overtones that should not be ignored. The entire edifice of slavery rested upon the assumption that the individual experiences of slaves did not matter. Otherwise, the carcasses of millions of potential slaves could not have been left floating in the Congo River by the slave ships that preyed upon Africa. Furthermore, a central component of the dehumanization brought by slavery was the depriving of the slave of access to language. If this is not clear enough from Toni Morrison's historically based portrayal of the use of the bit as a punishment for impudent slaves in her novel *Beloved*, [66]we might also remember that after Nat Turner's failed revolt, Southern states made it illegal to teach a slave to read and write. Similarly, we might remember the Abolitionist movement out of which comes the first type of African-American literature. The whole function of the slave narrative was to allow a slave to describe his personal ordeal. However, this portrayal was scripted for a political end by the Abolitionist movement. Thus, as John Sekora has pointed out in his essay "Comprehending Slavery: Language and Personal History in the *Narrative*," even the writer of the slave narrative was rarely able to write from the personal angle of his own experience.[67] Rather, he was presented as a slave, a type of human being worthy of compassion but incapable of planning and telling his own story. Only supremely gifted artists such as Frederick Douglass could create a compelling narrative of experience within the constraints of the slave narrative. Given this historical context, telling the story the way one experienced it, allowing the story to speak of one's particular experience must then be accorded a sacred place in the history of American letters.

A second and related issue is the notion of what is and is not a proper ancestor for a black writer. As an American writer, Ellison insists upon the freedom "to choose one's 'ancestors.'" "The World and the Jug" contains Ellison's self-selected list of ancestors: Hemingway, Malraux, Eliot, Dostoevsky, and Faulkner ("if you please or don't please!" Ellison adds, directly addressing Howe). Relatives, according to Ellison, cannot be chosen. Among these he lists Richard Wright and Langston Hughes, both of whom he insists are writers that he admires, but not writers from whom he traces his ancestry. He then attempts to explain why Hemingway's work is that of an ancestor: "Because all that he wrote—and this is very important—was imbued with a spirit beyond the tragic with which I could feel at home, for it was very close to the feeling of the blues, which are, perhaps, a close as Americans can come to expressing the spirit of tragedy."[68] The mixing of influences here is very important because it suggests a truly multicultural view of American literature at a time when multiculturalism was hardly a concept that one would find in an American literature classroom or anywhere else in American society. What is more, it does not suggest that Ellison is privileging white writers over black writers or mainstream writers over so-called minority writers.[69] In fact, it suggests just the opposite. If Hemingway can arrive at what Ellison defines as something akin to the blues without being black[70] and if the blues are "as close as Americans can come to expressing the spirit of tragedy," an art form that grew out of the culture of the fifth century B.C. in Athens, Greece, then American culture is not one stream but many. Both Hemingway and Leadbelly arrive at the same place by using diverse experiences and turning them into art. Thus, the artist defines his individuality not through class or race or even influence or a self-imposed lineage constructed of this or that canon but through intensity of feeling in relation to a self-selected and a self-described American experience. The source of that intensity of feeling may not be scripted from the outside; it must be lived, experienced, and chosen.

In this insistence upon the individuality of the artist and the freedom of choice that implies, Ellison does not deny the role of protest in art. He merely insists upon his own freedom to determine the nature of that protest: "The protest is there [in *Invisible Man*] not because I was helpless before my racial condition, but because I put it there." Further, he asserts again the moral role of the novel, insisting, "failing to be cognizant of social conditions" is "artistic immorality."[71] We should see here a consistency between the ideas that form the foundation of "The World and the Jug" and those we have seen in the earlier Ellison essays we have discussed. The novel grows out of experience, and it is the responsibility of the novelist to reflect accurately his or her experience of reality—thus the notion of confronting the reader with the crisis in American life or with the contradictions between the ideals of the Constitution and the realities of American life. But always that responsibility is personal. There is also broad consistency in other parts of Ellison's argument. Lawrence Jackson has shown in his *Ralph Ellison: Emergence of Genius*, that Ellison began emulating Hemingway's writing as early as 1935 while he was still at Tuskegee.[72] Such a fact suggests that Ellison's choice of Hemingway as an "ancestor" in this essay is in no way opportunistic or an endorsement of the status quo; rather, it reflects a long-standing affinity.

Ellison's insistence that he may choose his own ancestors, that other writers or thinkers may not impose the quality of his experience of oppression has created great controversy. First, in the increasingly politicized latter half of the twentieth century, to find a black writer who chooses as ancestors writers who all happen to be white is a rare phenomenon. Alice Walker claims to have been influenced by Flannery O'Connor. But in her description of her visit to O'Connor's home in *In Search of Our Mother's Gardens,* she has difficulty in separating the influence that O'Connor's work has had upon her from the reality of O'Connor's life as a white woman who was privileged to live a life that was materially better than that of Walker or her family. Walker chooses as ancestor Zora Neal Hurston, finding her grave and erecting a marker for it. According to Ellison's system, Walker would likely name O'Connor a relative, but not an ancestor in the same way that Ellison names Hemingway an ancestor. In similar fashion Toni Morrison began writing because, according to her, no one realistically addressed black life in fiction.[73] In short, she could find no literary ancestors. Morrison has also complained that she felt constrained and imaginatively diminished by "critical history," causing her to want to disavow the credentials the knowledge of literary history bestows.[74] The fact that Morrison holds a master's degree in English from Cornell suggests that she almost feels compelled to forget what she knows when she writes. On the other hand, Ellison argues that he consciously sought ancestors and that Hemingway arrived at something "very close to the feeling of the blues."

On a larger scale, Ellison's stance along with his longstanding reticence on civil rights issues has generated its own critical response and one wonders if the two have not been mixed by those who have tried to explain Ellison's work. "The World and the Jug" is a defense of art, a declaration of artistic integrity, a defense of individuality. Though Ellison does mention the "Negro Freedom Movement" and his responsibilities to it, he does so from the standpoint of an American writer. He claims to be "enlisted for the duration"[75] in the movement. But the role he claims within the movement is that of writer, not activist. What is more, he suggests that he must determine how to handle that role. Nonetheless, he freely admits his responsibility: "I took the time to question his [Howe's] presumptions as one responsible for contributing as much as he is capable to the clear perception of American social reality."[76] Despite these statements, later writers have tended to question Ellison's lack of involvement in the movement. Inescapably, these evaluations have colored the perception of his art and his writing about literature. Carol Polsgrove, in her recent book, *Divided Minds: Intellectuals and the Civil Rights Movement,* groups Ellison among those influential intellectuals who were notoriously silent throughout the Civil Rights movement. Jerry Gaffio Watts has written an entire book on Ellison's political silence, *Heroism and the Black Intellectual.* In discussing "The World and the Jug," Watts finds Ellison's rebuttal of Howe to be somewhat less than genuine: "In effect, by claiming that politics was merely one facet of black existence and perhaps not its most important component, Ellison is trapped into denying just how deeply the white treatment of blacks affected black life materially and psychologically."[77] Interestingly, Watts seems to reduce Ellison's argument to one that is based on politics and not on experience. Further, he seems to assume that Ellison seeks to characterize all blacks in his discussion of his own intellectual development. Ellison consistently returns to the particular experience as that which determines the quality of any writer's work, black or white. "Must I be condemned because my sense of Negro life was quite different [from that of Wright]?"[78] asks Ellison. To Howe's insistence that the novel is an "inherently ambiguous genre," Ellison insists that the "American Negro novelist is 'inherently ambiguous,'"[79] denying the existence of a prototype for black writers. To Howe's insistence that Wright presents representative black experience, Ellison responds: "But if you would tell me who I am, at least take the trouble to discover what I have been."[80] In every instance Ellison seems to insist upon the primacy of individual experience and to resist characterizing all black experience. So in answer to Watts's charge, we must remember that Ellison does not argue that politics has or has not deeply affected blacks. He argues that black experience is various and diverse, not easily characterized in sweeping statements such as those that we find in Howe or Watts. More to the point,

Ellison's main concern in "The World and the Jug" is the novel and the responsibilities that it foists upon the back of that man or woman who will be called writer. Whether Ellison should or should not be a part of the protest of the 1960s and later is a separate question.[81]

Still, if Ellison courageously defends the role of the artist in a way that is consistent with his definition of the novel, he does not completely answer Howe's evaluation of his novel. In fact, he pointedly ignores part of it. And it is this part of his argument that leaves questions. I pointed out in chapter two that many readers have found flaws with the end of Ellison's novel. I also argued in my own reading of the ending of the novel that though Ellison assumes that his narrator will leave the underground, that he has in some way reached the end of his quest, he never really explains how or presents a plausible notion of what he means when he writes, "there's a possibility that even an invisible man has a socially responsible role to play" (581). Howe also finds problems with the ending of *Invisible Man*, pointing specifically to the passage in the epilogue in which Ellison's narrator exclaims, "But my world has become one of infinite possibilities" (576). Howe explains: "Freedom can be fought for, but it cannot always be willed or asserted into existence. And it seems hardly an accident that even as Ellison's hero asserts the 'infinite possibilities,' he makes no attempt to specify them."[82] Howe exposes here a central gap in Ellison's thinking. While it may be possible to create novels or memoirs while living underground, can one assume that those novels create a more equitable society simply by exposing readers to the long gap between American ideals and American realities? Certainly, every piece of African-American writing since the slave narrative has attempted to expose to Americans the stark realities of black life, often to the contradictions in the words of the Declaration of Independence and the Constitution. Ellison's narrator escapes the realities of an invisible life by retreating into the infinite space of the imagination, but he does not figure out a way out of the hole. His catharsis is personal, despite the responsibility that Ellison feels that the novel and the novelist bear to society, despite what he calls his enlistment in "the Negro Freedom Movement."

The second essay that we will consider as a part of our examination of Ellison's focus on politics and art is "Hidden Name and Complex Fate." Originally an address delivered at the Library of Congress in 1964 that later was included in *Shadow and Act*, it ties some of the ideas that Ellison explores in "The World and the Jug" to those basic ideas of what the novel is and what the responsibilities of the novelist are that he had worked out in earlier essays. The subtitle to Ellison's essay is "A Writer's Experience in the United States," and clearly Ellison seems to be thinking again of the question of clear and opaque jugs. He begins the essay by referring again to Hemingway. He quotes from *Green Hills of Africa*: "Writers are forged in injustice as a sword is forged."[83] The whole question of injustice allows Ellison to turn again to the role that societal injustice plays in art. He states early in the essay that only through a writer's skill can "the personal and social injustice which he [the writer] suffered . . . lay claim upon our attention."[84] In the second part of the essay he moves into the argument that stands at the center of the response to Howe: the world that affects the writer. Ellison argues that even before a writer consciously plans to write, he absorbs the world around him. Ellison then provides for his hearers a two-and-a-half page catalog of experiences that he absorbed, ending with the remark, "There is much more, but this is sufficient to indicate some of what was present even in a segregated community to form the background of my work and my sense of life."[85] Following this catalog, he explains the literature that influenced him, once again listing a rather traditional canon of the Western writers, specifically mentioning Hardy, Eliot, Hemingway, Pound, and others. Though Ellison does state that "in my search for an expression of modern sensibility in the works of Negro writers I discovered Richard Wright,"[86] the catalog of literary influences in this essay is very similar to that which we find in other Ellison essays. In fact, he ends the essay referring to Henry James: "As Henry James suggested, being an American is an arduous task, and for most of us, I suspect, the difficulty begins with the name."[87]

The consistency in Ellison's ideas of the novel is again apparent. As it was in the National Book Award speech, the role of the novelist in Ellison's eyes is profound. He or she must strive "for the broadest range," discover and articulate "the most exalted values."[88] True to his insistence on the importance of individual experience, he adds: "And I must squeeze these [the range and values] from the life which I know best." [89] Then Ellison makes an extraordinary statement that returns us as readers to the title of the essay: "If all of this sounds a bit heady, remember that I did not destroy that troublesome middle name of mine; I only suppressed it. Sometimes it reminds me of my obligations to the man who named me."[90] Ellison refers here to his father who, as we discussed in chapter one, named him Ralph Waldo in hopes that he would become a poet. But in suppressing and not revoking or "destroying" that name, Ellison allowed himself in some ways to become the being that his father wanted him to be. Also, during an age when African Americans were discarding their American names in favor of new African names, Ellison insists upon his mixed identity, one that involves white people and white traditions as well as black people and black traditions, one that in itself embodies the whole notion of a "complex fate." We again see Ellison putting himself in a position that would lead to his being called an "Uncle Tom," accepting the name of a white man. But Ellison's essay refutes the logic of such a conclusion, for as in "The World and the Jug," Ellison insists that experience and fate are so complex and interwoven that names must always be ambiguous and many-sided, earned as well as given. Only as a particular individual may one discover the meaning and the fate that naming brings upon one.

Early in "Hidden Name and Complex Fate," Ellison quotes a black minister who exhorts his congregation, "we are our *true* names, not their epithets."[91] The play on words in this quotation is important to understanding Ellison's point. There is a kind of reciprocity in the name, but name is never fate. Name invites us to discover and to forge what we are by considering our experience of the world.[92] And considering our own experience and not that which is defined for us by others is the only way to earn one's identity. Speaking as a novelist, Ellison again insists upon the value of the particular experience in defining for the group a reality that has validity: "I feel that to embrace uncritically values which are extended to us by others is to reject the validity, even the sacredness, of our own experience. . . . It is a property and a witness which can be ignored only to the danger of the entire nation."[93] In short, the novelist is personally responsible for democracy and must seek to fulfill that responsibility by dealing honestly with his own experience as an individual. Thereby, he lives up to, defines, and even discovers his name, whatever that might be. Hemingway became Hemingway by the way in which he responded to and transformed his personal experience into art. In living up to his own name, Ralph Waldo Ellison will do likewise.

Ellison demands that the novel reflect American experience, that it reflect the American writer's personal responsibility for democracy, and that it set forth American identity. These concerns are hinted at as early as 1941 in a draft of "Richard Wright and Negro Fiction," one of his earliest pieces of literary criticism. They also appear in the last two essays he wrote exploring the role of the novelist: "The Novel as a Function of American Democracy" from 1967, and "Perspectives of Literature" from 1976. Ellison is astoundingly consistent in his choice of those writers who have fulfilled the responsibilities of the American novelist. The list almost always involves Melville, Hawthorne, Henry James, Twain, and Hemingway. But what might be more important than the consistency of Ellison's view of the novel is his dissatisfaction with the modern novel. Just as he alerts us to a "crisis" in the American novel in his National Book Award speech and in "Society, Morality and the Novel," so he returns to this issue again and again, particularly in "The Novel as a Function of American Democracy" and "Perspectives of Literature." America is a country that needs the novel in order to define itself, according to Ellison. In Ellison's eyes, contemporary American novelists have failed in this role: "If we do not know as much about ourselves now [as in earlier times], if we find that we read sociology and history more than we read novels, it is not our fault as readers. It is the fault of the novelist because he has failed his obligation to tell the truth, to describe with eloquence and imagination life as it appears from wherever he finds his being." [94] These are stark words for a man who was, as he wrote them, working toward completing a novel that he would never finish. Given the fact that Ellison considered his first novel his "not quite fully achieved attempt at a major novel," one wonders if he would have included himself in the list of those who had failed to provide the readers with what they needed to define themselves as Americans.

It is beyond the scope of this book to cover in detail all of the essays that Ellison wrote. Moreover, a book that attempted such would have space for little else besides Ellison the essayist. Nonetheless, it is important to note that Ellison wrote about subjects as diverse and many-faceted as jazz and painting and film and political figures. He was, to say the least, a prolific essayist whose interests were as broad as that range which he prescribed for the novelist in "Hidden Name and Complex Fate." Increasingly, scholars are paying attention to Ellison as an essayist. Two important studies of Ellison's work as an essayist have appeared in the last two years. Horace Porter's *Jazz Country: Ralph Ellison in America* (University of Iowa Press, 2001) and Robert O'Meally's *Living with Music: Ralph Ellison's Jazz Writing* (Modern Library, 2001) are indispensable guides for that student of Ellison who would understand the entirety of Ellison's work as an essayist, particularly as it relates to jazz. For us it is perhaps enough to know that though he only finished one novel, Ellison thought long and hard about the novel and its role both in his life and in the life of American culture. This thought became the source of some very important essays about the function and meaning of the American novel. Like Henry James and William Dean Howells, Ellison helped to define the American novel. Furthermore, when he turned to

other subjects, he often found at the heart of American culture the same
central concerns that he found at the center of the American novel. A few
examples will suffice to support this point. In "The Charlie Christian
Story" Ellison finds the "cruel contradiction" at the center of jazz to be
the very contradiction that seems inescapably the consequence of his
theory of the novel: the connection between the one and the many. "Each
true jazz moment (. . .) springs from a contest in which each artist chal-
lenges all the rest; each solo flight, or improvisation, represents (. . .) a
definition of his identity as individual, as member of the collectivity and
as a link in the chain of tradition."[95] In "Golden Age, Time Past," his
essay on the evolution in jazz from the Big Band Era to Bop, he applies
to the jazz artist much the same stipulation he places upon the back of the
novelist: the jazzman must find "his soul" in "that subtle identification
between his instrument and his deepest drives which will allow him to
express his own unique ideas and his own unique voice."[96] Finally, about
jazz greats such as Charlie Parker (the subject of "On Bird, Bird Watching and Jazz") and Jimmy Rushing (the subject of "Remembering
Jimmy") he can make the same observation that he makes about the
novel: "the abiding moods expressed in our most vital popular art form
are not simply a matter of entertainment; they also tell us who and where
we are."[97] Jazz, like the novel, is a part of that never-ending process of
defining and redefining what America is. And Ellison the essayist is forever seeking to understand who Americans are through looking at the
way our novels and our musicians define us.

  For Ellison the novel is a necessary part of American culture. Without
it, Americans cannot recognize the flaws in their culture; they cannot
define themselves. Without it, they turn their heads, are even justified in
turning their heads, according to Ellison. And yet as the twentieth century sped in chaos toward its confusing end, Ellison seemed to understand a darker truth: for all of his toil and for all of the toil of those like
him, America remained "an undiscovered country."[98] America and
Americans needed from the contemporary novel something that it never
provided for them. And perhaps in like fashion, America needed from
Ralph Ellison something he never provided: a fully achieved attempt at a
major novel.

Notes

1. Ralph Ellison, "Bearden," TCERE, 835.

2. Ralph Ellison, "The World and the Jug,"*TCERE*, 187-88. At another point in the same essay, Ellison makes a similar statement: "I think that the writer's obligation in a struggle as broad and abiding as the one we are engaged in, which involves not merely Negroes but all Americans is best carried out through his role as writer." Ellison, "The World and the Jug," *TCERE*, 178.

3. Ellison's meaning here is at best ambiguous. Earlier in the essay Ellison quotes Howe as saying the novel "is an inherently ambiguous genre: it strains toward formal autonomy and can seldom avoid being public gesture." Ellison's response to this quotation is as follows: "I would have said that it [the novel] is always a public gesture, though not necessarily a political one." Ellison, "The World and the Jug," *TCERE,* 158. Despite this statement, Ellison seems to imply at the end of the essay that he does consider at least his own novel writing to be a political act.

4. In a collaborative essay done by Ellison and James Alan McPherson, the writers recount Ellison's experience at Oberlin in 1969: "One girl said to him, 'Your book doesn't mean anything because in it you're shooting down Ras the Destroyer, a rebel leader of black people.'" After Ellison calmly responded, citing the fact that his book was almost twenty years old and it expressed only one man's opinion, "she went on to tell him, 'That just proves that you're an Uncle Tom.'" Ralph Ellison and James Allan McPherson, *TCERE,* 359. In a recent *American Masters* documentary on Ellison, Avon Kirkland interviews a witness to a much more disturbing encounter. At a reception following a reading, a young man arrived on a motorcycle to talk with Ellison. Before the entire company, he called Ellison an Uncle Tom, citing the ending of *Invisible Man* as evidence for the charge. Ellison responded by lowering his head and weeping on the shoulder of one of the guests, proclaiming softly, "I am not an Uncle Tom. I am not an Uncle Tom." Avon Kirkland, "Ralph Ellison," *American Masters*, PBS, February 21, 2002. Though this latter story clearly has the kind of sensationalism that makes a documentary exciting, John Callahan stated to me that this incident does not sound very much like the Ralph Ellison he knew. He describes a man who was very much focused on doing what he wanted to do, what he felt inspired to do, despite what any person, famous or otherwise, might have thought. According to Callahan, Ellison felt very much that in fulfilling the role of novelist to the best of his ability, he was fulfilling his role in the Civil Rights movement. This, of course, accords with what Ellison states at the end of "The World and the Jug." John Callahan, phone conversation with the author, May 8, 2003.

5. Ellison adds this statement to the above-quoted comments to Howe: "and here [in writing novels in answer to the demands of the "Freedom Movement"] I

am remiss and vulnerable perhaps." Ralph Ellison, "The World and the Jug," *TCERE,* 188.

6. In "On Initiation Rites and Power," Ellison describes the writing of *Invisible Man,* insisting that a part of the process was locating himself in the tradition of American literature: "I realized, fighting for a certain orientation (as a Negro writer who was taking on the burden of the American literary tradition), that I would have to master, or at least make myself familiar with, the major motives of American literature, *even when written by people who philosophically would reject me as a member of the American community."*

7. Lawrence Jackson, *Ralph Ellison: Emergence of Genius* (New York: Wiley, 2002) 312. Jackson's statement concerning "Richard Wright's Blues" clearly establishes the importance of the essay in terms of establishing a reputation for Ellison before *Invisible Man*: "His critique of Richard Wright's Black Boy, published in the summer issue of the *Antioch Review,* changed Ellison's career"

8. The doubtful reader might consult the collection of Ralph Ellison's papers at the Library of Congress. Many of the essays exist in draft after draft and many of the typed drafts themselves are heavily edited with pencil. Indeed, in many cases Ellison's papers show that he revised his essays as much as he did the episodes in *Invisible Man.*

9. Ralph Ellison, "Golden Age," *TCERE,* 241.

10. M. M. Bakhtin, *The Dialogic Imagination,* Ed. Michael Holquist, trans. Caryl Emerson and Michael Holquist (Austin: University of Texas Press, 1981), 9, 39.

11. Northrop Frye, "Specific Continuous Form," in *Approaches to the Novel* (San Francisco: Chandler, 1961), 43.

12. Richard Chase, *The American Novel and Its Tradition* (Garden City, N. Y.: Doubleday, 1957), 12.

13. Ibid., 12-13.

14. Emory Elliott et. al., *The Columbia History of the American Novel* (New York: Columbia University Press, 1991), xi.

15. Ibid., xi.

16. Bakhtin, *Dialogic Imagination,* 39.

17. Ibid., 6.

18. Ellison, "Hidden Name and Complex Fate," *TCERE ,* 205.

19. Ellison, "Brave Words for a Startling Occasion," *TCERE,* 154.

20. Northrop Frye, "Fictional Modes," in *Approaches to the Novel* (San Francisco: Chandler, 1961), 32.

21. Ibid., 32.

22. Bakhtin, *Dialogic Imagination,* 411.

23. Katarina Clark and Michael Holquist, *Mikhail Bakhtin* (Cambridge, Mass.: Harvard University Press, 1984), 348-350.

24. Ian Watt, "Realism and the Novel Form," in *Approaches to the Novel* (San Francisco: Chandler, 1961), 59.

25. It might be instructive at this point to remember Toni Morrison's statement concerning her relationship to the tradition of the novel: Stating that she does not want to be like "Joyce, Hardy, and Faulkner," Morrison says, "My effort is to be like something that has probably only been fully expressed in [black] music." Nellie McKay, Ed. *Critical Essays on Toni Morrison* (Boston: G. K. Hall, 1988), 1. Though no critic would jump to the conclusion that Morrison does not understand or participate in the tradition of the novel, it is clear that she consciously distances herself from the models of novel writing that have come before her. Ellison, on the other hand, seems always to locate his work in the tradition of major authors, quite often Faulkner and Twain.

26. Ralph Ellison, "Society, Morality, and the Novel," *TCERE*, 198.

27. Tying the phrase "human value" to morality is in no way a manipulation of Ellison's meaning given the title of the essay and the many times that Ellison mentions the concept of morality in this and other essays concerning the novel. Though I do not quote any of these here, this chapter is filled with examples of such statements.

28. Jean Stein, "Interview with William Faulkner," in *A Modern Southern Reader: Major Stories, Drama, Poetry, Essays, Interviews, and Reminiscences from the 20th Century South*, ed. Ben Forkner and Patrick Samway (Atlanta: Peachtree, 1986), 662.

29. Ralph Ellison, "Twentieth Century Fiction and the Black Mask of Humanity," *TCERE*, 92.

30. Ralph Ellison Manuscripts, Library of Congress, box 105, folder 2. Hereafter references to the Ralph Ellison Manuscripts at the Library of Congress will be abbreviated in this fashion: REM, LOC. Following this abbreviation I will insert the box and folder numbers.

31. Ellison, "Brave Words for a Startling Occasion," *TCERE*, 151. Early drafts of this essay do not include the word "personal" before "moral responsibility." This word is penciled in the typed copy of one of the later drafts, suggesting that Ellison thought carefully about what moral responsibility consisted of for a novelist. It is significant that he seemed to conclude that this responsibility was not a general concern with the future of American democracy but rather a very specific, personal concern with the fate of democracy. REM, LOC, box 170, folder 1.

32. Ibid., 153.

33. Ibid., 151. This line echoes almost verbatim the quotation cited above from the draft version of the 1941 essay "Richard Wright and Negro Fiction": "The future of the democracy is seen as wraped [sic] up in the development of the Negro" (REM, LOC box 105, folder 2).

34. Ibid., 153.

35. Ibid., 154.

36. Ibid., 151.

37. Ibid.

38. Ibid.

39. Ibid., 154.

40. Proteus was clearly an image that Ellison associated repeatedly with novel writing. On June 27, 1952, Hugh McGovern of the *Denver Post* sent Ellison some questions to be used to generate source material for a profile he was planning to do of Ellison for his newspaper. Among these questions was a rather standard request for information on literary influences. In Ellison's response, we find again the reference to Proteus with the same accompanying argument that he places with it in the National Book Award acceptance speech some six months later. Ellison even uses the same quotations from the *Odyssey* that we find later in the National Book Award speech REM, LOC, box 174, folder 10. A similar image appears again in the 1964 speech "Hidden Name and Complex Fate." Here Ellison uses the image of the Tar Baby as an emblem of the world. The writer becomes involved with this sticky figure, moving through stages of "playful investigation," then "labor," and finally "a fearful struggle, an *agon*." Ellison, "Hidden Name and Complex Fate," *TCERE,* 192. It seems clear from these examples that Ellison considers the role of the novelist to be one of struggle, and the nature of reality in these United States to be one of constant change. The writer thus grapples with a formless democratic reality in order to render up a shape or a form that we can identify.

41. Ellison, "Brave Words for a Startling Occasion," *TCERE*, 154.

42. Ibid.

43. We might recall here the defining qualities that Aristotle sets forth for deliberative rhetoric. As I pointed out earlier in our discussion of the political speech, Aristotle's category of deliberative rhetoric is always future-oriented, suggesting the way that things should be, not the way that they are or have been.

44. Ralph Ellison, "Brave Words for a Startling Occasion," *TCERE*, 154.

45. Ralph Ellison, "Stephen Crane and the Mainstream of American Fiction," *TCERE*, 123.

46. Ralph Ellison, "Society, Morality, and the Novel," *TCERE*, 694.

47. Ibid., 695.

48. Ibid., 697.

49. From its earliest usage in Athens during the fifth-century B.C., the word "rhetoric" has always been ambiguous. To some people it has meant the art of persuasion or, as Aristotle argues, finding the persuasive qualities in any given situation. To others, it has described the kind of chicanery that we associate with television advertising. It seems that Ellison uses the term in the former sense and not in the latter.

50. Ralph Ellison, "Society, Morality, and the Novel," *TCERE*, 697.

51. Ibid.

52. Ibid., 699.

53. Ibid., 701.

54. Ibid.

55. REM, LOC, box 106, folder 8.

56. The term "Black Boy" is not nearly as prejudicial as one might think. It alludes to *Black Boy*, Richard Wright's 1937 autobiography.

57. Irving Howe, *A World More Attractive: A View of Modern Literature and Politics* (New York: Horizon, 1970), 101.

58. Ibid, 112. It is worth noting that though Howe puts Wright's *Native Son* in the enviable position of the major African-American novel, he nonetheless finds flaws with it: "That *Native Son* has grave faults anyone can see. The language is often coarse, flat in rhythm, syntactically overburdened, heavy with journalistic slang" (104).

59. Ibid., 100.

60. Ralph Ellison, "Society, Morality, and the Novel," *TCERE,* 698.

61. Henry James, "The Art of Fiction," *The Portable Henry James* (New York: Penguin, 1979), 402. Earlier in the same essay, James defines the novel in a manner very similar to that of Ellison: "A novel is in its broadest definition a personal, a direct impression of life: that, to begin with, constitutes its value, which is greater or less according to the intensity of the impression" (394).

62. Ralph Ellison, "The World and the Jug," *TCERE*, 159.

63. Ibid., 170.

64. Ibid., 167.

65. The exact quotation here is important: "my pride lies in earning the right to call myself quite simply 'writer.' Perhaps if I write well enough the children of today's Negroes will be proud that I did, and so, perhaps, will Irving Howe's" (185).

66. The bit was a bridlelike iron implement that was placed around the neck of an impudent slave. A portion of the implement was fitted into the mouth and covered the tongue. When the bit was locked into place, it made it impossible for a slave to talk at all.

67. John Sekora, "Comprehending Slavery: Language and Personal History in the *Narrative,*" in *Modern Critical Interpretations: Narrative of the Life of Frederick Douglass*, ed. Harold Bloom (New York: Chelsea House, 1988), 154.

68. Ralph Ellison, "The World and the Jug," *TCERE*, 186.

69. "Do you still ask why Hemingway was more important to me than Wright? Not because he was white, or more 'accepted.'" (185)

70. In another passage in the essay, Ellison states that Wright is not capable of writing that approaches the feeling of the blues.

71. Ibid.,183;179-80. Ellison makes the latter statement in relation to Howe's contention that "Wright was perhaps justified" in ignoring changes that had occurred in the South in his novel *The Long Dream.*

72. Lawrence Jackson, *Ralph Ellison: Emergence of Genius* (New York: John Wiley and Songs, 2002), 147.

73. Susan Bakerman, "The Seams Can't Show: An Interview with Toni Morrison," *Black American Literature Forum* 12 (1978): 59.

74. Jan Stryz. "Inscribing an Origin in *Song of Solomon*" *Studies in American Fiction* 19, no. 1 (1991): 31.

75. Ralph Ellison, "The World and the Jug," *TCERE*, 187.

76. Ibid., 172.

77. Jerry Gafio Watts, *Heroism and the Black Intellectual* (Chapel Hill: University of North Carolina Press, 1994), 76-77.

78. Ralph Ellison, "The World and the Jug," *TCERE*, 166.

79. Ibid., 158.

80. Ibid., 163.

81. In point of fact, Ellison clearly states that protesting is not his responsibility as a novelist and that the writer who becomes a part of protest is not in any way improving his writing. When asked about advice for young writers in a 1965 interview with *Harper's Magazine*, he replied, "Beyond that, he [the young writer] shouldn't take the easy escape of involving himself exclusively in *talking* about writing or carrying picket signs or sitting-in as substitute activity. While he might become the best picket in the world, or the best sitter-inner, his writing will remain where he left it." Ralph Ellison, "A Very Stern Discipline," *TCERE*, 753.

82. Howe, 115.

83. Ralph Ellison, "Hidden Name and Complex Fate," *TCERE*, 189.

84. Ibid.

85. Ibid., 202.

86. Ibid., 204.

87. Ibid., 209.

88. Ibid., 208.

89. Ibid.

90. Ibid.

91. Ibid., 193.

92. In an effort to highlight some of the complexities and ironies of the "complex fate" that accompanies "hidden names" Ellison quotes his friend Albert Murray: "A small brown bowlegged Negro with the name 'Franklin Roosevelt Jones' might . . . turn out to be a hell of a fireside operator. He might just lie back in all of that comic juxtaposition of names and manipulate you deaf, dumb, and blind." Ibid., 194.

93. Ibid., 208.

94. Ralph Ellison, "The Novel as a Function of American Democracy," *TCERE*, 763.

95. Ralph Ellison, "The Charlie Christian Story," *TCERE*, 267.

96. Ralph Ellison, "Golden Age, Time Past," *TCERE*, 245.

97. Ralph Ellison, "Remembering Jimmy," *TCERE*, 277.

98. Ralph Ellison, "The Novel as a Function of American Democracy," *TCERE*, 763.

Chapter Four

Outside History

"Rinehart, baby, is that you?"
—Ralph Ellison, *Invisible Man*

Though Ellison ended his remarks at the funeral of his friend Romare Beardon by saying that "Art is the mystery that gets left out of history,"[1] I choose to begin this chapter by asking a question that in some respects turns Ellison's statement on its head: Can history be left out of art? Is it significant if a work of art fails to account fully for history or fails to predict the course history takes? Moreover, are these questions at all relevant to the art of the novel? Given the consistent connections that Ellison made between history and art in the statement quoted above as well as the famous statement from the National Book Award speech that the novelist is "personally" responsible for democracy, I contend that the issue is relevant to any serious study of the novel, in particular the politics of Ralph Ellison's novel writing.

Frederic Jameson's 1981 book, *The Political Unconscious,* is predicated upon a rather detailed analysis of the relationship between history and art. And though I in no way wish to invoke a Marxist approach to Ellison's work, such as that which Jameson follows in his own work, I do find certain of Jameson's ideas relevant to the politics of the novel. Drawing upon the work of Levi Strauss, Jameson argues that "the aesthetic act is itself ideological" in that its author presents "imaginary or formal 'solutions' to irresolvable social contradictions."[2] Thus, in the case of *Invisible Man,* Ellison is, as he has said, concerned with the problem of Negro leadership: "I was very much involved with the question of just why our Negro leadership was never able to enforce its will."[3] Consequently, his novel focuses upon a young man who would be a great leader of his people as Booker T. Washington was. As the young man ultimately fails in his quest, the novelist, through the voice of the young man, unravels the question of black leadership, articulating in the process a kind of statement of the problem that has never been formulated before. Because this statement of the problem exists in the form of a work of art, the statement itself could not exist in any other context. In essence, the ideology itself is inextricably bound to the nature of the artwork. As Jameson argues: "The issue here seems to be that the problem itself can only be recognized and stated in the text, that outside of the text it does not exist in a stated form in which it can be perceived as a clear contradiction and resolved: the text supplies the missing articulation and resolution to that articulation and conflict."[4] Thus, in the case of *Invisible Man*, Ellison articulates the problem of African-American leadership in a way that it has never been articulated before; to some degree this accounts for the novel's unprecedented success and importance in the context of twentieth-century American literature. Further, though his resolution is, as we have argued, tenuous, he does in some ways resolve the issue, leaving his invisible man free of all of those who would be his father, poised to come out of the underground, presumably to find a "socially responsible" role.

Still, given Ellison's high hopes for the novelist, given his lofty conception of the form, which we explored in chapter three, can we assume that articulation and resolution as an ideological act is enough? Must there be some inherent relationship between history and art, so that the novelist points the way toward the reality of what history will be or at least accounts for history? Jameson's system does not allow the work of art to be an ideological act that exists in a vacuum. Jameson asserts that the work of art must be viewed in the context of three concentric horizons: that of political history, that of society and class struggle, and that of history, or what he calls "modes of production." The last of these is the all-encompassing context of events as they happen. In Jameson's terms, "History is . . . the experience of Necessity, and it is this alone which can forestall its thematization or reification as a mere object of representation or as one master code among many others."[5] In a similar statement later in the work, Jameson writes: "History is what hurts, it is what refuses desire and sets inexorable limits to the individual as well as collective praxis."[6] Jameson argues that history is what happens rather than what we would hope or imagine might or should happen. It is the ultimate horizon, the ultimate reality that forever frames what we would imagine or create for those who come after us. Thus, Harriet Beecher Stowe's novel *Uncle Tom's Cabin*, published in 1852, is forever associated with the Civil War, which began in 1861. It is in light of this ultimate "horizon" of history that I wish at least briefly to examine Ellison's work.

At the end of chapter two I asserted that Ellison's invisible man, who is left contemplating his reentry into society, his return from the hibernation that has lasted too long, must be viewed in the context of the social upheavals that occurred in the 1950s and 1960s. Ellison's novel appeared in 1952, and some three years later, in December 1955, the bus boycotts in Montgomery, Alabama, began the painstakingly slow process of transforming the way in which Americans viewed color. Furthermore, the painstaking way in which this change was effected drew on resources within the black community that are not at the forefront of the resolution that Ellison finds for the conflict in black leadership in *Invisible Man*. Public speech, which Ellison's narrator rejects for a time in favor of writing, became the focal point of the Civil Rights movement in the eloquent speeches of Martin Luther King, Jr. Indeed, King's "I Have a Dream" speech is arguably the most important as well as the most well known speech of the twentieth century. It is also some of the most familiar television footage of the twentieth century. Furthermore, what we might call the cult of personality, with various leaders jockeying for position, much as Ras the Exhorter and Ellison's narrator jockey for position in *Invisible Man*, became a matter of front-page news and is now a part of the historical record. In this regard we should not only think of the well-known conflict between Martin Luther King, Jr., and Malcolm X but also conflicts within the Southern Christian Leadership Conference between Martin Luther King, Jr., and Ralph David Abernathy. We might also remember the conflict between the Southern Christian Leadership Conference (hereafter referred to as SCLC) and the Student Nonviolent Coordinating Committee (hereafter referred to as SNCC), which resulted finally in the birth of the Black Power movement. All the while, J. Edgar Hoover was bent on politically assassinating Martin Luther King, Jr., and arranged this attempted character assassination with the help of a reluctant attorney general, Robert Kennedy.[7]

These elements of chaos form a part of the given reality of our culture. More important for us in this study is the foreground of the picture: the collective voice of black people without which neither the Civil

Rights movement nor the Black Power movement could have existed at all. Both of these movements drew upon the power of the black community to band together rather than to seek to define itself in individualistic terms. Both of these movements thrived on the spoken word. And as the movements developed, they relied increasingly upon the media coverage that they began to garner. In Jameson's terms, these historical details are the ultimate horizon of events. The crisis in black leadership would not be solved by the act of a novelist or even by the collective acts of many novelists. The crisis in black leadership would be solved by a group effort carefully orchestrated so that the persuasiveness of its rhetoric (often in spoken form) became impossible to resist. And as with most rhetorical victories, this one occurred in a context rife with the very conflict and chaos that Ellison's narrator flees from at the end of *Invisible Man*. Furthermore, in a twist of fate that is peculiar to the twentieth century, the rhetorical context of the Civil Rights movement cannot be understood without taking into account the role of the media.

For all of the narrator's rejection of public speech at the end of *Invisible Man*, despite his spearing of Ras and finding himself in losing his identity as a public speaker, there is a sense in which Ellison's narrator is aware of the very power of at least some of the forces that would begin the slow process of societal change. Buried in his experience at the funeral of Tod Clifton is an awareness of what ultimately works as well as an awareness of what does not. After the narrator's speech, which, as I argued in chapter two, works by understatement and is in many respects antirhetorical,[8] the narrator recognizes its failure: "I had let it get away from me, had been unable to bring in the political issues. And they stood there sun-beaten and sweat-bathed, listening to me repeat what was known" (459). But earlier, at the opening of the funeral, the narrator recognizes the power of the song "Many Thousand Gone" "aroused" by an old man in the audience. The power of the song enables the group to become one whereas at the end of his speech the narrator can only see "the set faces of individual men and women" (459).[9] It is no coincidence that the narrator feels a "twinge of envy" when he looks at the singer, for the song arouses the very collective response the narrator fails to get. Certain words that Ellison's narrator chooses suggest that the song may provide an answer to the question which the narrator poses when he looks at the crowd gathered to mourn the departed brother: "could politics ever be an expression of love?" (452). The narrator muses concerning the old man who sings, "It was as though the song had been there all the time and he knew it and aroused it, and I knew that I had known it too and had failed to release it out of a vague nameless shame or fear. But he had known it and aroused it" (453). Similar statements could have been made about the song that became and remains the anthem of the Civil Right movement, "We Shall Overcome." The song captured the collective feeling of discontent and merged it with the demand for change, so that politics indeed became, at least for those in the movement who sang it and continue to sing it, an expression of love. And "We Shall Overcome," like "Many Thousand Gone," is a spiritual that came from the collective past of black people, not the expression of an individual artist writing from underground. It is a song that grew out of and perpetuates the call and response tradition that demanded not a lone singer, but a singer and a chorus of people who joined in the singing at pivotal points in the song.

Ellison seems to have been aware of the centrality of this scene in *Invisible Man*. Fourteen years after the publication of the novel, Whit Burnett contacted Ellison, requesting a selection for the quarter century Doubleday publication, *This Is My Best*. Subtitled "America's greatest living authors choose their own best work," this publication was made up of selections that an author chose as quite literally the best he or she had ever written. Whit Burnett wrote to Ellison: "In 1942 I did not have the pleasure of writing you to ask you to select something from your work for THIS IS MY BEST of that period. I have the pleasure now, for your readers have spoken—and voted—and you are among the most often nominated for inclusion in the new THIS IS MY BEST OF TODAY."[10] Ellison chose for his "best" the scene from *Invisible Man* describing the funeral of Tod Clifton. In explaining his choice, Ellison himself alludes to the very force that would be central in the Civil Rights movement, tying it to politics. According to Ellison, the scene in question is *peripetia*, in that it reverses the direction of the plot of *Invisible Man*. In organizing the funeral and speaking to the assembled mass, the narrator has attempted to politicize the death of Tod Clifton in order to enable the Brotherhood to regain lost influence in Harlem. His failed speech becomes the focal point of his attempt. In the process of recognizing his own failure and the success of the song, he discovers what he has in common with Harlem. Ellison writes in his explanation of this scene:

Thus, he [the narrator] is forced willy-nilly back upon himself and upon that which he shares most irrevocably with the people of Harlem i.e., to those ritual and ceremonial forms taken from the Protestant tradition which Negro Americans had begun to structure to their own religious and cultural needs as far back as the early days of enslavement, and which recently were to be observed most movingly during the funeral ceremony for Martin Luther King. [11]

In short, the narrator's speech at the Tod Clifton funeral fails, but the traditions of the black church invoked by the occasion and more specifically by the song succeed.

In large measure, these very traditions became the foundation of the Civil Rights movement. Furthermore, these are the very traditions that the narrator seems most remote from in the epilogue to *Invisible Man,* for despite his desire to serve "a socially responsible role," he is alone, crafting a tale that expresses the torment of one invisible man. "Many Thousand Gone" and "We Shall Overcome" were the stories of many men and women written by a writer so little concerned with his or her individual creation that an author's name does not even survive with the song. Ellison's narrator is likewise "invisible," but he pointedly complains of this fact in the prologue to the book. In fact, a part of the narrator's device in the novel is to create the individuality that we associate with a name and then not supply the name. There is no sense in which Ellison or his narrator seeks the anonymity of the author of the ballad or folk song or the spiritual. But in order to understand just how remote Ellison's narrator is from these traditions, we must briefly examine the Civil Rights movement itself.

The Southern Christian Leadership Conference (SCLC), the political organization most closely associated with the Civil Rights movement, set out to redeem the soul of the nation,[12] and its success or failure in this endeavor is still a matter of conjecture. However, the Civil Rights movement transformed American society, and the SCLC and its most eloquent spokesperson, Marin Luther King, Jr., were at the forefront of that process of change. What is more interesting for our study is the haphazard welter of events out of which the movement came and through which it existed and succeeded. Martin Luther King, Jr., did not come to Montgomery, Alabama, in order to start the Civil Rights movement. Very much like Ellison's invisible man at the scene of the eviction in Harlem, he simply found himself moved to speak at the pivotal moment. And again like Ellison's invisible man, he exercised his considerable talent to move an audience, drawing on those traditions in which he as a minister was steeped.[13] More important, what grew out of his speaking and organizing was a curious mixture of the native eloquence of the black church and the careful orchestration of some of the most skilled rhetoricians in the business, organization which ultimately appealed to the national media. Indeed, just as Ellison's narrator in *Invisible Man* and Ras the Destroyer use the oldest snake oil in the business—rhetoric—so did King and his organization. Understanding this complex array of events takes us back to where we began this study: the art of speaking, as Aristotle and those who came after him understood it.

I argued in chapter one that the difference between Aristotle and Plato in their approach to rhetoric is basically that Aristotle understands the practical necessity of rhetoric whereas Plato is always bothered by the fact that rhetoric and truth do not always coincide. Thus, Aristotle opens his treatise on rhetoric with the famous statement that rhetoric is the "counterpoint of dialectic."[14] On the other hand, Plato, speaking through the mouth of Socrates, warns us that rhetoric is related to truth in the same way that cookery is related to nutrition—it merely makes whatever happens to be put forth by the speaker palatable to the audience. Thus, if the man skilled in rhetoric wishes to make something other than the truth palatable, then rhetoric will also serve him well.[15] One sees a similar dichotomy between the novel *Invisible Man* and the Civil Rights movement. King seems to have been increasingly aware of the practical necessity of rhetorical strategies and flourishes and public speech whereas Ellison's invisible man seems finally paralyzed by the demands of truth, demands that ultimately drive him underground, "torturing myself to put it down" (579). The central question that has lingered in the wake of Ellison's achievement is in reality the one that Ellison's narrator asks from the underground: Can he indeed "speak for you" and what finally does this statement mean?

King's becoming the most famous and influential spokesperson for the Civil Rights movement is hauntingly like Ellison's invisible man's rise as a speaker in Harlem. Like Ellison's fictional character, King just happened to be on the scene at the pivotal moment that the Civil Rights movement began, and also, like Ellison's character, he aroused the audience using the call-and-response pattern that is such a familiar part of the black church. Taylor Branch in *Parting the Waters*, his Pulitzer-Prize-winning account of the first seven years of the Civil Rights movement, describes King's election as president of the Montgomery Improvement Association, the predecessor to the famed Southern Christian Leadership Conference. After Rosa Parks was arrested for violating the segregated seating laws governing city buses in Montgomery, Alabama, E. D. Nixon, former president and nominal leader of the local chapter of the NAACP, called King, pastor of the Dexter Avenue Baptist Church, and asked for his endorsement of a bus boycott. King did not readily agree to the endorsement, though he did agree to allow a group meeting about the matter to use his church that afternoon. By the time the meeting began, King had agreed to endorse the boycott. Less than a week later, King's late arrival at a meeting at Holt Street Baptist Church concerning the boycott was pivotal in his becoming president of the newly founded Montgomery Improvement Association. King walked into the church just as E. D. Nixon was delivering an excoriating attack on the other black ministers present for their refusal to back the boycott openly. According to Branch, an angry Nixon said: "Let me tell you gentleman one thing. You ministers have lived off these wash-women for the last hundred years and aint never done nothing for them."[16] He then demanded that they stand up and "be mens." King's response to this taunt was as follows: "Brother Nixon, I'm not a coward, . . . I don't want anybody to call me a coward."[17] A moment or so later, Nixon nominated King as the first President of the Montgomery Improvement Association. Since no other nominations were forthcoming, Martin Luther King, Jr., became the organization's first president.[18] In turn, that organization became the foundation of the Southern Christian Leadership Conference, the organization that would set out "to save the soul of the nation."

King's power over his audience was also hauntingly like that of Ellison's character in *Invisible Man*. Even though King came to Dexter Avenue Baptist Church as he was moving toward completion of his Ph.D. in theology from Boston University, his success with his audience was often based upon his intuitive grasp of the traditions of the black church, the pattern of call-and-response speaking that relies heavily upon audience involvement. As we explored in chapter two, Ellison's narrator's speech at the Harlem eviction, as well as his first Brotherhood speech in *Invisible Man* places the speaker in close proximity to the audience. The speech he gives at the funeral of Tod Clifton distances him from the audience because it contains none of the audience repartee that characterizes the first. The narrator's success as well as his sense of well-being in both of the earlier speeches is based upon audience response. In the Harlem eviction speech, the narrator hits his stride when he riffs upon the word "dispossessed" that a member of the audience uses.[19] In the first of the Brotherhood speeches, the audience is also intricately involved in the shaping of the speech. When the narrator asks the audience for "a chance," an audience member responds with "'We with you, Brother. You pitch 'em, we catch 'em!'" (342). As the speech develops, the narrator is constantly asking the audience for a response in exchanges such as this one:

"Tell me if I'm right."
"That's a strike, Brother." (342)

King's first speech as president of the Montgomery Improvement Association was similar to both of these speeches in that it sprang to life when the speaker began interacting with the audience by using the call- and-response tradition.

The speech occurred at Holt Street Baptist Church on the same day that King was elected President of the Montgomery Improvement Association. Taylor Branch reports that the first part of the speech only brought forth a mild response from the audience. During this portion of the speech, King recited the facts of the case that had brought forth the boycott and discussed the impeccable character of Rosa Parks. But the speech really began to achieve lift when King hit upon the catch phrase of the evening: "And you know, my friends, there comes a time, . . . when people get tired of being trampled over by the iron feet of oppression."[20] Using the classic rhetorical device of anaphora, King clung to the phrase "There comes a time when people get tired of . . ." in much the same way that Ellison's narrator uses the word "dispossessed": "There comes a time, my friends, when people get tired of being thrown across the abyss of humiliation, where they experience the bleakness of nagging despair."[21] Branch describes the audience response in this fashion: "The giant cloud of noise shook the building and refused to go away. One sentence had set it loose somehow, pushing the call-and-response of the Negro church service past the din of a political rally and on to something else that King had never known before"[22] (139-40). If indeed the response of the audience was something that King had never experienced before, it seems likely that he had achieved the very feat that Ellison's narrator despairs of achieving at the end of the Tod Clifton eulogy in *Invisible Man*. At that moment, Ellison's narrator feels "through the haze" the tension. What is more, he recognizes that it is a power that must be put to constructive use: "something had to be done before it simmered away in the heat" (461). If for a moment we allow history and literature to intermingle, we might imagine that on that real evening at Holt Street Baptist Church three years after the publication of *Invisible Man*, King had indeed discovered that "something" that would allow the tension to do more than simmer—with one amazing phrase, Martin Luther King, Jr., had brought the tension to a boil.

This approach to speaking was not something that was confined to King's early speeches or relegated to those speeches that he gave to audiences that were primarily black. Indeed, the "I Have a Dream Speech" itself was very much an outgrowth of the call-and-response tradition that King knew in his bones rather than the theological education that he had received at Boston University and other elite schools. In contrast, the entire organization of the March on Washington reflected the careful orchestration of forces that we see in Ellison's narrator's planning of the funeral for Tod Clifton. The organizers wanted to achieve maximum influence, just as Ellison's narrator wants to regain influence in Harlem. Civil Rights activist Bayard Rustin carefully limited the time of each speaker at the Lincoln Memorial, insisting "that a hook-man would unceremoniously yank them from the podium if their speeches exceed seven minutes."[23] Branch notes that a part of the motivation for this plan was the desire to "refute the racial stereotype of imprecision and inbred, self-indulgent tardiness."[24] King also planned his speech with great care. However, it was not the planned portion of the speech that would be remembered or that would transform America. Taylor Branch describes the text of the planned speech as "far from historic."[25] But interestingly, King abandoned the text late in the speech when he began quoting the Old Testament prophet Amos.[26] Thereafter, in the words of Branch, King had "no alternative but to preach."[27] But what to preach caused King to stumble. According to Branch, Mahalia Jackson, sitting on the podium behind King, urged him on: "Tell 'em about the dream, Martin." [28] No one knows whether King heard these words. King only stated later that he picked up the first line of oratory that occurred to him.[29] Still, even if King did not respond directly to Jackson's comment, the "I have a dream" sequence of the speech had been nurtured not in the libraries of Boston University but in black churches across the country, for it was a segment of a speech that King had delivered many times, a riff of sorts that he was accustomed to using.[30] Taylor Branch effectively describes the irony of the situation: "It was a fitting joke on the races that he [King] achieved . . . statesmanship by setting aside his lofty text to let loose and jam, as he did regularly from two hundred podiums a year."[31] Thus, like Ellison himself, King recognized the power of the rhetoric of call-and-response, of the black church, of the black sermon tradition itself. But unlike Ellison's narrator at the eulogy for Tod Clifton, he allowed it to infiltrate his words.

Though King had certainly made inroads in national circles before the March on Washington, the "I Have a Dream Speech" opened new doors for him. President Kennedy himself, watching the speech from the White House, commented to staffers, "He's damned good." He greeted King a few moments later with the tag phrase from the speech, the tag phrase that came from the pulpits of black churches and would from then on be a part of American history, "I have a dream."[32] King had essentially given a speech that, like Booker T. Washington's famous "Atlanta Exposition Address" (the model for Ellison's narrator's first speech in *Invisible Man*), had created a national response. But unlike Washington's speech, King's speech had rejected accommodation and insisted upon a new day of equality for African Americans. Unlike Ras the Destroyer or Malcolm X, King's plea was not based upon separation or violence—it was very much what Ellison's narrator had envisioned at the funeral of Tod Clifton, politics as an expression of love. It had also drawn upon the basic traditions of black culture, traditions that Washington did not use in his speech. Finally, it was the first step in a process by which black leadership would finally be able to accomplish what Ellison had claimed to be concerned with in *Invisible Man*, namely, "enforce[ing] its will."[33] It is the very kind of speech that we would assume Ellison's invisible man might have made were he not constrained by the Brotherhood to follow the "scientific approach," had he not ducked into the underground, had he ever come out of the underground. It drew upon those same forces that Ellison seems to have been intensely aware of in both *Invisible Man* and *Juneteenth*: the power of the black church and its traditions, the power of the African-American community and its traditions, the unrecognized genius and brilliance of black people and black language, but most of all the native power of speech, specifically African-American oratory. If we can again allow history and literature to mingle, King embodied in many respects the solution to that question that bothered Ellison as he delved into the writing of *Invisible Man*: the question of black leadership. King would be the black leader who would transform American culture. But ironically, though the power of his rhetoric might have created a national debate, the slow process of change did not come about just because of King's speaking. Rather, it grew out of the careful organization of people like Bayard Rustin. With the organizational skills of a Brother Jack and the jockeying for position of a Ras the Destroyer and the many disguises of a Rinehart, they played the rhetorical game with enormous skill, pitting one group against another, seeking advantage and position. They did not do this from the cold, clear light of the underground, but from the welter of voices that was very much like the politically charged, ethically compromised, burning streets of Harlem from which Ellison's character escapes in order to define himself.

The actions in Birmingham in 1963 constitute a clear example of organizational politics, of playing the angles, of strife-torn streets and absurdity. King and his company played games much like those of Rinehart, becoming invisible when necessary and reappearing at a moment's notice, wearing a new mask. The Civil Rights Movement was a brilliant combination of voice, passion, politics, and skill. As King grasped intuitively, it grew out of the ethical core of American character, but it was not conducted from a place of solitude and reflection. In fact, as matters developed, there was hardly time for people like King to remember who they were and what they were about.

By the time King came to Birmingham early in 1963, some five years had passed since the bus boycotts. The "I Have a Dream" speech on the Washington Mall was four months away. Though King was widely admired by his audience and widely despised by bigoted southerners, his reputation in the media and among Civil Rights old-timers was at best ambiguous. The code name for him among the media was Mahatma. Reporters following the Civil Rights movement were regularly told to "Go where Mahatma goes." King was a potential martyr to be exploited by the media. Editors and producers figured that he might get killed, and they wanted to be first to cover the story. Every member of the media wanted him to be his or her own martyr.[34] Meanwhile, younger members of the movement, some of them members of SNCC, called King "De Lawd," ridiculing his large following among the more emotional members of the movement. They also objected to what they perceived to be his elitism—his expensive attire, his seeming reluctance to work long and hard in the trenches. King and his organization had yet to initiate a protest movement. They had only reacted to events in cities such as Montgomery, Alabama, or Albany, Georgia. The most recent demonstrations in Albany were by and large a failure. According to Diane McWhorter, Birmingham minister and SCLC member Fred Shuttlesworth expressed the doubt that many members of the black community had concerning King. She quotes him as saying to King: "We've got to move in Birmingham, . . . We've been hammering away for seven years with no impact."[35]

Even after King followed Shuttlesworth's advice and came to Birmingham to initiate a protest, he succeeded not by virtue of his famed "Letter from a Birmingham Jail"[36] or even his well-honed speaking style. The movement succeeded in Birmingham because of the media. To some extent the SCLC and its organizers were able to play the media, but on another level, the media played the movement much in the same way that the Brotherhood used Harlem and the narrator of *Invisible Man* to create a riot. McWhorter argues that the Albany demonstrations had failed because Albany police chief Laurie Pritchett had refused to react to the demonstrations with violence. Bull Connor, Birmingham's chief law enforcement officer, provided the kind of violence that would create media attention. According to McWhorter, "The real lesson of Albany was that nonviolence could not succeed without violence—segregationist violence."[37] King and his movement found violence in Birmingham, but even then "enforce[ing] its will" (as Ellison despairs of black leaders being able to do) was a matter of enormous complication.

King's going to jail in Birmingham (the stay that would produce "The Letter from a Birmingham Jail") was carefully orchestrated. Not only was the stay in jail planned but also it was timed. In first arriving in Birmingham a week before Easter 1963 to start the protest, King thought that he would go to jail early and thereby encourage others to join him. When it became clear that his organizational and negotiating skills were needed outside of jail,[38] King sent others to jail, including his brother A. D. King. Both King and Ralph David Abernathy wore Liberty Overalls instead of their usual expensive suits in order to appear to be one of the people. King even told an audience: "I will wear them [the overalls] as long as I am in Birmingham and until we are free,"[39] something he of course did not do unless we assume that the movement attained freedom for blacks just after King's jailing in Birmingham. As the Birmingham movement began to look more and more like a second Albany, McWhorter reports that King continued his coalition building and stayed out of jail. Then came the pivotal blow. Bull Connor and the Birmingham police asked for and received from Judge William A. Jenkins an official decree forbidding King and any in his organization from planning or participating in a public demonstration. Already having planned his demonstration and potential jailing to coincide with the passion of Christ, ("I can't think of a better day than Good Friday for a move for freedom," he told an audience.[40]), King suddenly was facing a showdown with state law even though that law deprived him of his constitutional right to assemble and demonstrate.

Though King stated publicly: "I am prepared to go to jail and stay as long as necessary,"[41] there is plenty of evidence that he had his doubts. His father, the famed minister Daddy King, told him not to march.[42] Fred Shuttlesworth later said "I am sure that had I not been in Birmingham, he would not have marched. My position was forthright and almost came down to an ultimatum."[43] Whatever the state of King's resolution, King did march and did go to jail, but only after a rather public retreat into private for prayer, perhaps consciously echoing Christ's prayers in the Garden of Gethsemane. Still, though the trip to jail coincided with Easter and produced the eloquent "Letter from a Birmingham Jail," it did not produce the hoped-for outpouring of support from the Birmingham community. Blacks in Birmingham did not want to join King in jail. Nor did these incidents play the way the Civil Rights movement operatives wanted them to in the national media. Criticized by the Kennedy administration and most national media, the SCLC's actions in Birmingham produced nothing until King got out of jail. It was then in desperation that civil rights organizer Jim Bevel suggested to King that they jump-start the Birmingham initiative by encouraging children to march in the streets and be arrested. This plan was backed by Andrew Young and later by King himself.[44]

From the vantage point of the twenty-first century, it is easy to see how brilliant the so-called Children's Campaign was, but to many at the time, it seemed at best reckless, at worst opportunistic. It was in essence the same type of rhetorical strategizing that Ellison's invisible man finally flees from. Ellison's character tries and fails to make a martyr of Tod Clifton. He repents of both this action and all other political opportunism when he realizes that the Brotherhood seeks to use any number of martyrs—Tod Clifton, himself, Ras, the entire Harlem community—to achieve its end of overthrowing the power structure in the United States.[45] King had to choose to make a martyr of himself for media consumption, and then when that did not work, he was forced to make martyrs of the black children of Birmingham. The important distinction between King's movement and the Brotherhood's is, of course, the nature of the causes. King's cause was holy and just, politics as an act of love, whereas the Brotherhood's cause had at its center a revolutionary political agenda. King was nonviolent; the Brotherhood was willing to use violence to further its agenda. Despite these differences, the means of achieving the end is eerily the same. The group must play politics, sacrificing the identity, sometimes even the life of the individual. King ultimately played the role of martyr so well that he and the part became one. He willingly gave his life, and every American is in his debt for that. But that event was five years away. In the meantime he used the children of Birmingham as martyrs. And even then, the fact that it worked at all was only a trick of luck and the media or some strange combination of the two.

The children's march began on May 1st, a day on which as many as 800 black children chose to march and go to jail rather than go to school. Well-known black Birmingham businessman A. G. Gaston pleaded with King to let the children stay in school.[46] By May 3rd, the number of students who missed school had nearly doubled to 1,500. The children marched in the street in waves and sang movement songs. When the police approached them, they knelt to pray as they had been taught to do and were willingly led away to jail. By Sunday, May 5th, the crowd was between one and three thousand.[47] Just as the strategists had hoped, the children's martyrdom had inspired their parents in a way that King could not. As the crowd sang, the music of the black church was once again infectious. Much like the singing of "Many Thousand Gone" at Tod Clifton's funeral, the effect was so profound that as in *Invisible Man*, whites were singing too. Dubbed "Miracle Sunday" by later commentators, May 5th of 1963 would go down in history as a day that defied easy explanation. Promising the violence that he was famous for and that the movement ironically needed, Bull Connor had called out the fire department to hose down the marchers. With the jails full, he could not arrest them all. Movement participants contend that the firemen were so moved by the marchers and their singing and chanting that they simply refused to obey his order.[48] Historians Branch and McWhorter further contend that the police and the firemen refused to hinder the marchers as they strode through their ranks, singing "I Got Freedom over My Head." Both Branch and McWhorter describe this moment using the same metaphor, rich in echoes of the black church.[49] The line of policemen and firemen parted "like the Red Sea," McWhorter states.[50] "Nonviolence had touched the fireman's hearts, they [the demonstrators] said, and had tamed Bull Connor's hatred as surely as Moses had parted the Red Sea," writes Branch.[51]

Despite the way in which the marchers had affected Birmingham officials, the "freedom" that King called for was still not achieved. The "I Have a Dream" speech and the March on Washington were still three months away, not to mention the fact that even those events would not bring "freedom" or even an immediate Civil Rights Bill. But curiously the cause was furthered enormously by a photograph that proved to speak much louder than even King's eloquence or the so-called movement songs. Probably the most famous photograph of the Civil Rights movement, the picture shows a black youth and a police dog in violent confrontation with one another. The dog is being restrained by the police officer, and the black youth seems to be reacting with classic nonviolence, his hand held loosely at his side. Bill Hudson of the Associated Press took the photograph, and on Saturday, May 4, 1963, it appeared on the front page of papers across the nation, including the all-important *New York Times*. President Kennedy publicly claimed to be sickened by it, as did much of the rest of the world outside of Birmingham.[52] Ironically, the so-called demonstrator was actually Walter Gadsden, a bystander who was crossing the street. His pose of nonviolence was the natural reaction of a man who has been attacked by a dog. He raised his knee to keep the dog away, holding his hands by his side, presumably to keep them out of the dog's mouth. Walter Gadsden's desire not to demonstrate was so profound that thirty years after the event when Diane McWhorter tried to interview him, he responded by refusing and saying that "he didn't want to 'get involved.'"[53] Nonetheless, according to McWhorter in *Carry Me Home*, this photograph was pivotal in swaying the country in the direction of the movement. Taylor Branch in *Parting the Waters* also attests to the power of this particular photograph, stating: "President Kennedy, like millions of readers, could see nothing else."[54] McWhorter goes even further: "The K-9 Corps of Birmingham took its mystical place next to the bloodhounds chasing Eliza across the ice floes in *Uncle Tom's Cabin*." Ellison's narrator in *Invisible Man* learns from Rinehart that identity is fluid matter; wearing sunglasses and a hat can allow one's true identity to become completely invisible. In walking across the street at just the right time, Walter Gadsden seems to have lived out that fictional moment. In common terms he inadvertently pulled a Rinehart and became the ultimate demonstrator confronting the ultimate embodiment of the unrepentant South: a snarling German shepherd. And if McWhorter and Branch are to be believed, it was hardly coincidental that within the next two years, black leaders would in a true sense of the word "[enforce] their will." King would give the most famous speech of the twentieth century, he would win the Nobel Peace Prize, and Lyndon Baines Johnson, a Southern politician who had come into politics as a segregationist, would maneuver the long-awaited Civil Rights Bill through the Senate. In so doing, he acted out the wishes of the slain John Fitzgerald Kennedy. No one would argue that civil rights were achieved by these acts, but despite that fact, black leaders had done what Ellison despaired of them doing as he wrote *Invisible Man*. They had enforced their will.

Since history never comes to us with meanings attached, understanding any series of events is always a matter of conjecture, guessing at causes and effects, weighing evidence to draw a conclusion. Thus Diane McWhorter draws the conclusion that the photograph of Walter Gadsden was comparable in its effect on the Civil Rights movement to the effect of Stowe's *Uncle Tom's Cabin* on the Civil War and more specifically the emancipation of the slaves. Though proving McWhorter's statement (if possible at all) is beyond the scope of this study, the idea does shed some light on the politics of novel writing in the twentieth century. Published exactly one hundred years before Ellison's *Invisible Man,* Stowe's novel sold 10,000 copies in the first week and 300,000 by the end of its first year.[55] Within two years it had sold two million copies. The novel produced such a politically charged response that fourteen proslavery novels appeared by 1855, all purporting to rebut Stowe's portrayal of slave life. Stowe responded to the questions concerning her accuracy by publishing in 1853 *A Key to Uncle Tom's Cabin,* producing facts that corroborated her portrayal of slavery. All of these events make quite understandable Abraham Lincoln's famous statement upon meeting Stowe for the first time: "So you are the little lady who started the big war." [56] More important, Lincoln supposedly reread *Uncle Tom's Cabin* just before he announced the Emancipation Proclamation in 1863.[57]

In light of the nature of this study, in light of Jameson's ideas with which this chapter began, these facts are quite significant. In the case of the Civil War and the Emancipation Proclamation, there is clear evidence that literature did indeed become an important part of the context of historical events or, to use Jameson's term, the political horizon. In chapter three we discussed in detail the fact that Ellison insisted upon the novel's moral role in shaping democracy, a moral role that he associates with the nineteenth-century American novel. The National Book Award speech contains the famous line, "Indeed if I were asked in all seriousness just what I considered to be the chief significance of *Invisible Man* as a fiction, I would reply: its experimental attitude, and its attempt to return to the mood of personal moral responsibility for democracy which typified the best of our nineteenth-century fiction."[58] Stowe apparently did take personal moral responsibility for shaping democracy, so much so that she fashioned a novel to resemble history and verified the details of her portrait. In so doing, she became a part of history, shaping significantly the slavery debate that was tearing away at the conscience of the nation. Ellison apparently saw in *Invisible Man*, which he modestly called "my not quite fully achieved attempt at a major novel,"[59] the same attempt but

with quite different results. In its conclusion at least, Ellison's final portrait of his invisible man stands in conflict with the real horizon of historical events. Black leaders in this country would not enforce their will
by retreating to the underground and writing novels or even going to jail
and writing letters from therein. They would enforce their will through
speech and through manipulating the very forces that manipulated them.
And when the tide of the battle was finally turned, it would be in the
hands of a kind of latter day Rinehart, a man who was photographed appearing to be what he was not, to bring the nation to attention. But even
if Ellison's novel had been more in tune with the actual tone of events,
one wonders if it would have allowed its author to take "personal moral
responsibility for democracy." Novels about civil rights seem to have
had relatively little to do with "saving the soul of America" if that soul
has even yet been saved. These novels were powerful and profound in
their ability to shape the intellectual communities in America. In fact,
one might even attribute to them the long overdue emphasis that we have
seen on race and gender in universities over the past twenty years. But in
terms of shaping public policy, a much more important element of democracy, novels seem hardly able to compete with media coverage.[60]

Even if we look only at the reading population of the country itself,
the story seems to be the same. What were Americans reading during the
decades of the 1950s and the 1960s? Though *Invisible Man* was a best-
seller and a winner of the National Book Award, it was not one of the ten
best-selling books of 1952. In fact, no work of fiction by an African
American was among the best-selling ten books of the year for any of the
years between 1950 and 1970. During that twenty-year period, only two
novels dealing substantively with race are among that yearly group of
ten: Harper Lee's *To Kill a Mockingbird* in 1962 and William Styron's
The Confessions of Nat Turner in 1967.[61] In striking contrast, in the first
year of its publication, Harriet Beecher Stowe's *Uncle Tom's Cabin* was
the best-selling novel in the history of American literature. Clearly, if
numbers of readers can be considered an indication, novels about race
were not stirring the national consciousness concerning race in the way
that Stowe's novel ignited the sparks that would bring about the Emancipation Proclamation. If McWhorter's comparison is correct, the media
played a more important role than the novel in weaving the fabric of democracy.

Ellison's narrator in *Invisible Man* asks of Rinehart, "Could he be
both rind and heart?" (498). Though such a question might forever puzzle the reader of *Invisible Man* given Rinehart's many mysterious identi-

ties, a similar question asked about the photograph of Walter Gadsden need not puzzle us. He was used for his rind and not for his heart, for his heart was miles away from the demonstrations in Birmingham. And the media that came to Birmingham looking for a martyr found one in Gadsden's rind if not in his heart. Thus, Ellison's novel was correct in its portrayal of reality—Rineharts are all around us, particularly in the riot-torn streets of America's cities. But it was not correct in the conclusions that it seems to draw. Shaping the nature of reality would not be left up to those who wrote novels. That job would be passed along to the preachers and the rhetoricians and the photographers and those who chanced to walk among them. And Ellison's next novel would be taken over by one of those preachers, but Ellison himself would be unable finally to move from a "not quite fully achieved attempt at a major novel" about black leadership to a fully achieved attempt. The next novel would find him laboring for forty years and still not quite figuring out how to take "personal moral responsibility for democracy."

Notes

1. Ralph Ellison, "Bearden," *TCERE*, 835.

2. Frederic Jameson, *The Political Unconscious: Narrative as a Socially Symbolic Act* (Ithaca, N. Y.: Cornell University Press, 1981), 79.

3. Ralph Ellison, "On Initiation Rites and Power," *TCERE*, 525.

4. Jameson, *Political Unconscious*, 79.

5. Ibid., 98-99.

6. Ibid., 102.

7. This bizarre story of sex, scandal, and squalor has been recounted in various places. In essence, Hoover used his knowledge of sexual liaisons involving JFK in order to "persuade Robert Kennedy that wire tapping King was in order." The interested reader is directed to Taylor Branch's account in *Parting the Waters* (New York: Simon and Schuster, 1989), 566-68, or Diane McWhorter's account in *Carry Me Home* (New York: Simon and Schuster, 2001), 298-99.

8. Of this passage, Ellison writes to Whit Burnett, "I like the reverse-English rhetoric of the sermon itself." By "sermon" Ellison refers to the eulogy delivered by the narrator. REM, LOC, box 164, folder 8.

9. Ellison's narrator observes: "Even white brothers and sisters were joining in" (453).

10. REM, LOC, box 164, folder 8.

11. Ibid.

12. Diane McWhorter, *Carry Me Home* (New York: Simon and Schuster, 2001), 307.

13. Though these are not the precise traditions out of which Ellison's narrator grows, he certainly recognizes and appreciates their power in scenes such as the speech of Homer Barbee or the funeral of Tod Clifton. On the other hand, these *are* the very traditions that produce Alonzo Hickman, the subject of the next chapter of this book.

14. Aristotle, *The Art of Rhetoric*, Trans H. C. Lawson-Tancred (London: Penguin, 1991), 66.

15. Plato, *Gorgias,* in *Readings in Classical Rhetoric.* ed. Thomas W. Benson and Michael H. Prosser, trans. W. R. M. Lamb, (Davis, Calif.: Hermagoras Press, 1988), 19.

16. Taylor Branch. *Parting the Waters: America during the King Years* (New York: Simon and Schuster, 1989), 136.

17. Ibid., 137.

18. Several other facts make this event rather interesting. Shortly before the Rosa Parks arrest, Branch reports that King had expressed to his wife and mother his desire to run for president of the local chapter of the NAACP. Both women had advised him not to do so. They did not think that he had time for the job with a new baby and a new church to tie him down. When he proposed the idea to E. D. Nixon, King encountered another serious obstacle. Nixon had already thrown his support to another candidate. Thus, whatever political ambitions King might have had, it seems unlikely that he walked into the boycott meeting seeking the presidency of a newly formed organization. Branch's reading of King's election gives credence to my characterization of it as haphazard. He argues that an idealist would see King's election as an outcome of his gifts whereas a realist would see it as the result of his being new in town and having few "debts or enemies." The cynics would assume that it was a simple lack of wisdom; the older, more established ministers knew better than to put themselves in such a dangerous position. Whatever the case, it seems clear that King did not come to Montgomery, Alabama, in order to start a movement of any kind (Branch, *Parting the Waters*, 137).

19. "'Dispossessed?' I cried, holding up my hand and allowing the word to whistle from my throat. 'That's a good word. Dispossessed! Dispossessed, eighty–seven years and dispossessed of what? They aint got nothing, they caint get nothing, they never had nothing. So who was dispossessed?'" (279).

20. Branch, *Parting the Waters,* 139.

21. Ibid., 140.

22. Ibid., 139-40.

23. Ibid., 873.

24. Ibid.

25. Ibid., 875.

26. Interestingly, the passage that King quoted was supposedly his favorite passage of scripture (Branch, *Parting the Waters*, 141), a sentence that is now inscribed on the Civil Rights Monument that sits one block away from Dexter Avenue Baptist Church in Montgomery, Alabama. The inscription on the monument reads: "Let justice roll down like water, and righteousness like a mighty stream." Amos 5:24.

27. Branch, *Parting the Waters*, 882.

28. Ibid.

29. Ibid, 182.

30. In her Pulitzer Prize-winning book *Carry Me Home*, Diane McWhorter notes that a civil rights activist named Charles Davis taped King speaking at the Sixteenth Street Baptist Church in Birmingham during April 1963. A portion of that evening's speech included the repeated phrase, "I had a dream tonight." Diane McWhorter, *Carry Me Home* (New York: Simon and Schuster, 2001), 335.

31. Branch, *Parting the Waters*, 887.

32. Ibid., 883.

33. Ralph Ellison, "On Initiation Rites and Power," *TCERE*, 525.

34 . McWhorter, *Carry Me Home*, 308.

35. Ibid., 307.

36. According to Diane McWhorter, "It [Letter from a Birmingham Jail] would not be published in full for nearly two months [after the Birmingham marches], and it became a sacred civil rights document only in the afterglow of Birmingham" (355).

37. Ibid., 308.

38. Ibid., 327.

39. Ibid., 328.

40. Ibid., 341.

41. Ibid., 342.

42. Ibid., 345.

43. Ibid., 346.

44. Ibid., 363.

45. Thus, we have the narrator's famous statement of recognition: "Use a nigger to catch a nigger." This statement occurs moments before the spearing of Ras, the event with which this book began.

46. McWhorter, 367.

47. Though establishing exact numbers is impossible, I am relying on those used in McWhorter's *Carry Me Home,* 370–87.

48. This fact is confirmed in both McWhorters's *Carry Me Home* (387) and Branch's *Parting the Waters* (767).

49. According to Dolan Hubbard in *The Sermon and the African American Literary Imagination,* "Let my people go" is the most important mascon in the traditional black sermon.

50. McWhorter, *Carry Me Home*, 387.

51. Branch, *Parting the Waters*, 768.

52. Ibid., 764.

53. McWhorter, *Carry Me Home*, note on 375.

54. Branch, *Parting the Waters*, 764.

55. Establishing a comparison here is rather important. The best-selling novel in the history of American literature prior to Stowe's *Uncle Tom's Cabin* was Lippard's *The Quaker City*. It sold 200,000 copies. Since Stowe's novel sold a third more than this number during its first year, it is clear that its success was beyond belief. Emory Elliott, *The Columbia History of the American Novel* (New York: Columbia University Press, 1991), 54.

56. Robert E. Spiller and others, *Literary History of the United States,* rev. 3rd ed. (New York: Macmillan, 1973), 563.

57. Barbara Smith, "Harriet Beecher Stowe: 'A Little Bit of a Woman,'" *Literature Study*, Third Floor Publishing [cited July 19, 2002]; Available at www.chfweb.com/smith/harriet.html.

58. Ralph Ellison, "Brave Words for a Startling Occasion," *TCERE*, 151.

59. Ibid.

60. Perhaps this sad state of affairs explains Ellison's comment later in the National Book Award speech: "That my first novel should win this most coveted prize must certainly indicate that there is a crisis in the American novel. You as critics have told us so, and current fiction sales would indicate that the reading public agrees" Ellison, "Brave Words," 151.

61. "1950s Bestsellers" and "1960s Bestsellers," available: www.caderbooks.com/best50.html and caderbooks.com/best60.html, respectively.

Chapter Five

Juneteenth:
The Coon Cage Eight and the Joe Cah

"Hear me out: I say that even the wildest black man rampaging the streets of our cities in a Fleetwood knows that it is not our fate to be mere victims of history but to be courageous and insightful before its assaults and riddles."
Senator Sunraider's speech on the floor of the Senate
—Ralph Ellison, *Juneteenth*

Posthumous novels have always been in a class by themselves. Even when they are published exactly as the writer left them, the reader must always wonder in what state the writer left them. Wide variations in the working habits of writers make the problem hopelessly complex. Some writers revise a first or second or third or fourth draft heavily and others may revise as they go, giving to a first or second draft a kind of validity it might not have coming from the hand of another novelist. Finally, there is literary history itself, which warns the careful reader that he or she should beware giving too much credence to posthumous material. Mark Twain's *The Mysterious Stranger* is a famous example of what might happen to those manuscripts that a writer leaves. Published in 1916, some six years after Twain's death in 1910, Albert Bigelow Paine, Twain's biographer and literary executor, purportedly pieced together three manuscript versions of the story, discovering Twain's ending for the novel among some fragments and unfinished stories that he left. The

113

novel was read and admired as Twain's final work, even touted by Bernard DeVoto as Mark Twain's come back "from the edge of insanity."[1] Then John S. Tuckey demonstrated in 1963 that Paine had misdated the manuscripts. Further research revealed that Paine and Frederick Duneka of Harper's Publishing had, in the words of Fred Gibson, "cut and bowdlerized the manuscript heavily."[2] What appeared to be Twain's final work on the novel was not Twain's work, and, more important, what most people took to be Twain's final conclusions about what he called "the damned human race" were not his final conclusions. The lesson here is one that every biographer, literary executor, textual critic, and literary critic must take very seriously. One must tread lightly indeed when working with something other than the author's final intentions. In such a context all conclusions are at best tenuous.

Ralph Ellison's literary executor, John Callahan, seems to have approached what Ellison left with a very light tread. First, the manuscripts that he dealt with were apparently quite extensive and quite heavily revised and emended. Given the fact that Ellison labored for forty years on the text in question, even determining the state of the manuscripts was a rather large order of business. In a 1999 interview with Christopher De Santis, Callahan states that Ellison's so-called second novel was in actuality a conglomeration of writings: "I was working within a necessity that there be one novel, period. A single, coherent, continuous novel. And it struck me that, whatever Ellison's intentions and hopes had been, that wasn't what he had done. What he did was to leave fragments—some extremely fragmentary and others all but complete—of several potential novels or narratives within his saga."[3] Callahan decided to publish the most coherent unit in the manuscripts and the one that he found central to all of the manuscripts left at Ellison's death. As he says in the introduction to *Juneteenth*, "this [the narrative comprising *Juneteenth*] was the center of Ellison's great, unfinished house of fiction."[4]

Despite Callahan's care, one must recognize that he did indeed make a choice among the manuscripts that Ellison left. *Juneteenth* might or might not have been what Ellison considered the center of his forty years of unfinished work. According to Callahan's calculations, most of what now makes up *Juneteenth* was book II of the unfinished second novel. Though it was conceived in the late fifties, Callahan said in a conversation with me that his examination of the manuscripts and Fanny Ellison's dating of the manuscripts lead him to believe that Ellison continued to tinker with this portion of the book off and on, until at least 1986.[5] We can only speculate what it was about the story of Hickman and

Bliss/Sunraider that intrigued, perplexed, and eluded Ellison for thirty years. Likewise, we can only wonder why Ellison chose finally not to publish some book-length version of what Callahan calls an "all but complete" novel. Despite these questions and reservations, Callahan's light tread does suggest, to me at least, that the novel should be given some measure of credence. Callahan's editorial project was completed at the request of and with the approval of Fanny Ellison, the person who was presumably closer to Ellison than anyone else. What is more, Callahan is insistent that his role in the novel was to select and copyedit the portion of the manuscript that was to be the posthumous novel and then entitle it *Juneteenth*. De Santis pursues this question doggedly in his interview, quoting Callahan's statement in the afterword to *Juneteenth*: "I felt uneasily procrustean: Here and there limbs of the manuscript needed to be stretched, and elsewhere a protruding foot might be lopped off."[6] In response to De Santis, who asks if he "added words to the manuscript" or "stitched together pieces," Callahan says: "Neither of the above."[7] Thus, *Juneteenth* is Ellison's work and deserves to be treated as such. Nonetheless, given the nature of this study, two questions must inform or frame our discussion of it. First, why was Ellison not content to publish it, particularly as he moved toward what he must have known would be his last years? Second, given the fact that Ellison chose not to publish it, how should one fit the book into the context of Ellison's work as a whole? In short, how should it be read, particularly in the context of the politics of Ralph Ellison's novel writing?

Since Ellison died in 1994, there can be no final answer to the first question. To my knowledge, Mrs. Ellison has not spoken publicly about this matter.[8] Furthermore, those who have spoken provide no information that seems to explain this fact. John Callahan, who knew Ellison well, calls it a complicated question to which there is no simple answer.[9] In a recent documentary on Ellison, Albert Murray, Ellison's close friend, contends that toward the end of Ellison's life, Murray simply could not bring up the second novel around Ellison.[10] In a rare television interview with Bryant Gumbel in 1982, celebrating the thirtieth anniversary of the publication of *Invisible Man*, Ellison blamed the delay for the second novel on the fire at the Plainville home, a fire that burned much of the manuscript.[11] In his introduction to *Juneteenth* John Callahan gives a very complete account of Ellison's public comments on the novel in progress as well as the comments of friends. Still, no clear answer to this question emerges. In fact, Ellison seems at times quite contradictory. Late in his life Ellison blamed the famous fire at the Plainfield home for the loss of "a good part of the book."[12] Yet in 1980, some thirteen years after the fire and two years before the television appearance with Bryant Gumbel, Ellison told a reporter "I guess I've been able to put most of it back together."[13] To complicate matters more fully, these comments are all general, dealing with what Ellison called the second novel, a conglomeration of manuscripts that according to Callahan is several thousand pages long. None of these comments addresses specifically what is now *Juneteenth*.

Ellison did, however, allude to what is now *Juneteenth* in his 1982 interview with writer John Hersey. Ellison clearly refers to two details from *Juneteenth* in this interview and dates his use of these details to 1956, the period during which he was a fellow at the American Academy in Rome.[14] He states that the novel at least began with the idea of a "Negro evangelist" who used a child rising out of a coffin as a part of his evangelizing and that a part of the basic situation was a political assassination treated comically. The first part of Ellison's statement undoubtedly refers to Alonzo Hickman's evangelistic trick of putting Bliss in a coffin and having him rise up at a pivotal point in the sermon. The second likely refers to the assassination of Sunraider, the beginning of *Juneteenth*. What is more interesting perhaps is Ellison's statement a moment later in the interview affirming that the Kennedy and King assassinations years later "slowed down the writing."[15] These statements suggest that Callahan is quite correct in placing the incidents in *Juneteenth* at the center of Ellison's "house of fiction." If the political assassination was central to the project in the late fifties and then also in the early and late sixties, we must assume that it occupied a central position in Ellison's vision of the work. This also underscores Callahan's contention that Ellison continued to tinker with this portion of the novel until at least 1986. Further, Ellison's statement implies that current events might have had something to do with Ellison's decision not to publish the novel. This latter observation should be qualified, however, by Ellison's statement at another point in the Hersey interview: "I am terribly stubborn, and once I get engaged in that kind of project, I just have to keep going until I finally make something out of it."[16] The picture that emerges here is one that is quite intriguing. We have a writer who doggedly sticks to his original idea; forty years devoted to one book would certainly testify to Ellison's tenacity. But we also have a writer who, at the very least, understands his work in the context of current events.

Such an observation takes us back to one of the central ideas that we discussed in chapter four, namely, the relationship between history and art. If we read *Juneteenth* in the context of the "political horizon" that existed when it was conceived, we must place the novel in the America of the 1950s. Thus, though there may never be an answer to our first question of why Ellison did not publish the novel, we can in part answer the second question. Alonzo Hickman and Bliss/Sunraider were conceived in the late fifties at the very time that Martin Luther King, Jr., and the Montgomery Improvement Association were beginning the bus boycotts. But if Ellison continued to change the text until 1986, we must assume that this is in no simple way a fifties novel. Indeed, according to John Callahan, the only person outside of Fanny Ellison who has seen the entirety of the manuscript of the second novel, this novel addresses the time period "before the great change"; it is a novel about a time "on the cusp of change." Callahan contends that if *Invisible Man* is a novel set in the context of segregation, then *Juneteenth* is a novel set in the midst of the change that would bring integration.[17] Thus in reading the novel, we must tie it not only to the fifties, an era that might have produced Alonzo Hickman and Senator Sunraider, but also to the sixties and later. Though Ellison set the novel in the fifties, the characters continued to evolve as he worked on the narrative. Clearly, connections to the Civil Rights movement were in Ellison's mind, for they appear in some of the notes that he took on the novel, notes that Callahan includes in an addendum to the published text.[18] Ellison writes in one note: "Action takes place on the eve of the Rights movement, but it forecasts the chaos which would come later."[19] At another point, he writes: "Bliss rejects Christianity as sapping of energies, Hickman sees it as a director of energies. In this he foreshadows Martin Luther King, while Sunraider repeats the betrayals of the past."[20] At another point in the notes we find another possible allusion to King: "One of the implicit themes at work here is Hickman's refusal to act politically, his refusal to use politics as an agency for effecting change. And at this point we enter the historical circumstances of the fifties wherein Negro ministers become overtly political through the agency of passive resistance."[21] In contrast, Hickman has hoped to effect change in a nonpolitical fashion. In another note, Ellison writes, "Hickman has staked a great part of his life on the idea that by bringing up the boy with love, sacrifice and kindness, he would do something to overcome the viciousness of racial division."[22] The striking matter concerning these notes is how consistently they seem to revolve around the involvement and the noninvolvement with politics.

Hickman's approach to the evils of racism is to try to solve these matters entirely with an act of love. He will raise the abandoned child whose father is unknown, despite the fact that the child's very existence brought about the destruction of his own family. Still, his act is not entirely devoid of political calculation. He hopes that Bliss, the product of his love and devotion, will become a great politician in the lineage of Lincoln. Sitting at the bed of the dying Sunraider, Hickman remembers his recent visit to the Lincoln Memorial and reflects upon Lincoln's life. At this moment he cannot help but connect what he had hoped Bliss would become to what lies before him in the dying Sunraider: *"And to think,* Hickman thought, stirring suddenly in his chair, *we had hoped to raise ourselves that kind of man."*[23] Thus, the actual mixing of politics and love is something that Hickman can effect only through an emissary, not through the direct force of his own eloquence. Ellison's invisible man asks at the funeral of Tod Clifton if politics can ever be an act of love. His trip underground seems at least for a time to suggest that it cannot. The same issue of mixing politics and love seems to haunt Ellison as he conceives the characters and events that might have comprised his second novel had he chosen to publish it. And once again, as we find in the closing pages of *Invisible Man*, there seems to be no clear answer to that question. *Juneteenth* is ultimately about the failure of Hickman's dream rather than its realization.

Martin Luther King, Jr., went to Washington, D.C. in August 1963 in order to stand on the steps of the Lincoln Memorial and demand those rights and privileges that had been denied to people of color. He brought with him a multitude of the disenfranchised as well as those who championed their cause. Standing on the steps of the Lincoln Memorial, before the enormous seated figure of Lincoln, King made a speech that would call attention to the one hundred years that had passed since Lincoln had signed the Emancipation Proclamation, a hundred years that had included an endless record of betrayal and discrimination, of promises unfulfilled and even forgotten. Hickman's trip to Washington at the beginning of *Juneteenth* has interesting similarities to and differences from that of King. If we assume that Ellison wrote this section of the novel in the fifties, the scene anticipates King's trip and King's speech in uncanny ways. But if we assume that Ellison continued to revise this portion of the second novel until 1986, we must wonder if the scene did not take on a special resonance in terms of the actual events of King's life, in particular the canonizing of the "I Have a Dream" speech as one of the most important speeches of the century. A novel that begins with the whole

notion of African-Americans going to Washington and demanding recognition of any kind would seem in the fifties almost prophetic and
thereafter it would be impossible to use the scene without alluding to
King's speech. Furthermore, in bringing his congregation with him, in
taking them to the Lincoln Memorial to visit "Father Abraham," Hickman brings to the seat of so-called justice a microcosm of the disenfranchised people whom King fought for, the very people who would stand
and hear him speak at the Lincoln Memorial in 1963.

Still, Hickman's trip to Washington, with congregation in tow, is astoundingly different from King's. It is motivated not by a desire to protest the dream deferred or even to forestall the evil political machinations
of Sunraider, his former protégé and potential emissary. It is motivated
by a desperate attempt to keep Sunraider alive, despite his racism.[24] Even
as Sunraider is shot, Hickman responds with absolute grief that forces
him to sing, "Oh, Lord . . . why hast thou taken our Bliss, Lord? Why
now our awful secret son, Lord?" (38). A more overtly political figure
would have recognized that, though the assassination is tragic and wrong,
the silencing of bigotry on the floor of the Senate would certainly be politically expedient to all of those African Americans ignored and abandoned by the American political process. Hickman never draws this conclusion concerning the event, even as he sits philosophically at the bed of
the dying Sunraider. In fact, even before the assassination, Hickman refuses to mourn the tragedy of Sunraider's desertion of those who raised
him. When Sister Neal chokes back tears in the Senate gallery, exclaim-
ing that Sunraider is using speaking techniques that he picked up from
Hickman in order to brandish about his racism, Hickman states simply
"Don't, Sister Neal, ... This is just life; it's not to be cried over, just
understood" (34). Though different in age and occupation from the narrator of *Invisible Man*, Hickman ultimately makes two choices that Ellison's invisible man would understand. He chooses to seek a way of
combining politics and love, and he chooses ultimately to seek understanding over passion, analysis over direct political involvement. Ellison's invisible man writes, "In going underground, I whipped it all except the mind, the mind. And the mind that has conceived a plan of living
must never lose sight of the chaos again which that pattern was conceived" (580). Interestingly, both of these choices, like those of Ellison's
invisible man, keep Hickman out of the realm of politics.

Despite the clear connections between *Invisible Man* and *Juneteenth*,
it is extremely important to distinguish between the two.[25] Though
clearly fruitful, such an approach obscures the profound differences be-

tween the two narratives, in particular the allegory that seems to be at the center of *Juneteenth*. If we remove *Juneteenth* from the topical events of the fifties and sixties, if we expand the political horizon, we suddenly see the grand allegory at the center of the novel, an allegory that applies not to the mid-to-late twentieth century alone, but to all of American history. Alonzo Hickman is indeed "God's trombone," for he personifies the quiet patience of all African-Americans as they have waited for the Declaration of Independence and the Constitution to be applied to them, the patience that has enabled them to shape American culture and then watch quietly and without violence as it turns its back on them and declares itself a beacon of independence and self-reliance, shaped by and for white Americans. Bliss/Sunraider is that independent, self-reliant American, imbued with the resourcefulness and courage that enable him to be first an evangelist, later a moviemaker and finally a senator. But in spurning those who nurtured him, he obscures the fact that he has no real history apart from them, that he has no real culture apart from them, that he is of them as they are of him. In essence, the novel dramatizes one of Ellison's central perceptions: that Americans are not white or black—they are both. As Ellison's invisible man learns from Lucious Brockway at Liberty Paints, the white cannot exist without the black. Thus, what was lost when Ellison chose not to finish or publish the narrative associated with *Juneteenth* might have been the great epic American novel that confronts the politics of race through a kind of allegory of American history. If fully developed and explored, the allegory at the heart of *Juneteenth* might have been as rich and as evocative as the metaphor of invisibility in *Invisible Man*. Had it been published in the fifties at the onset of the Civil Rights movement or in the sixties as the movement began to bring about change, it might have indeed rivaled Stowe's *Uncle Tom's Cabin* in its ability to shape democracy at a pivotal point in time. But since the novel was never finished or published, we will never know exactly what it might have been. Appearing in 1999 after the high points of both the Civil Rights movement and the Black Power movement had passed, it seems at times, as some reviewers have noted, dated.

Still, thanks to John Callahan's tireless work, we have a remnant of what might have been and with that we can perhaps understand the direction in which Ellison was heading. And if this was indeed to have been the epic American novel on race and politics, we see that Ellison's vehicle for confronting these issues was public speech. The entire book is an extended rumination on the lives of two profoundly gifted speakers and two men who between them illustrate the double edge of rhetoric. The

trip from Bliss to Sunraider is in part a rhetorical one, and if it takes us
from unalloyed virtue and innocence to vice, it also takes us from the
sermon at its best to the political speech at its worst, the very two forms
that we explored in chapter one.

Sunraider's speech on the floor of the Senate early in the novel is a
savage parody of political rhetoric. In fact, it is so savage a portrayal that
one wonders if Ellison would have allowed it into a published edition of
book II without toning down its excesses. The vacuity of windy preachers and posturing politicians has rarely been parodied to this extreme.
Ellison's narrator prepares us for this tour de force by having Senator
Sunraider "in the gay and reckless capriciousness of his virtuosity" (13)
seek quite literally to shatter the windowpanes of the Senate chamber.
There follows rhetorical posturing such as the following: "Time flows
past beneath us as we soar. History erupts and boils with its age-old con-
tentions. But ours is the freedom and decision of the New, the Unclut-
tered, and we embrace the anguish of our predicament, we accept the
penalties of our hopefulness. So on we soar, following our dream" (15).
Like so much political rhetoric, these words expose the ability of language to stand somewhere between fiction and fact. No one could dis-
agree with these words because they have no real concrete substance.
And yet they are imbued with force through the very power of their imagery, through its very connection to cherished American ideals and
symbols such as freedom and soaring eagles. Sunraider's rhetoric reaches
its fever pitch as well as its point of absolute absurdity when he proposes
"quite seriously" the renaming of Cadillac "this fine product of American
skill and initiative" the "Coon Cage Eight." He reasons that "its initial
value" has been diminished by its being frequently seen in Harlem holding "eight or more of our darker brethren crowded together enjoying its
power" (23). As the Senator follows this with more vacuous rhetoric—
"For we— . . . —by the grace of Almighty God, are A-MERI-CANS!"
he is shot by his son Severen who stands in the Senate Gallery (24).

This scene echoes unmistakably the spearing of Ras the Destroyer at
the end of *Invisible Man*, the very scene with which this book began. Ras
also is silenced in the midst of a rhetorical posture as he calls for the
hanging of the narrator of *Invisible Man*. In fact, we might almost conclude that once again Ellison seems to be beginning this novel where he
ended the previous one. Still, there are important and obvious differences. The spearing of Ras takes place at the end of *Invisible Man* and
thereafter we never see Ras again. The shooting of Sunraider takes place
at the beginning of *Juneteenth*, and the rest of the novel is in part a trip

back in time, an exploration of what Bliss was, of the roots of the rhetoric that we see Sunraider so shamelessly brandishing on the floor of the
Senate. But in both novels, the practitioner of political rhetoric is silenced in mid gesture.

Due to the incomplete nature of the novel and also due to its modern-
ist aesthetic, we do not fully understand the journey from Bliss to Sunraider. We know basically that Bliss was the child whose very existence
brought about the lynching of Hickman's brother as well as the death of
Hickman's mother. We know that Hickman named him Bliss *"because
they say that's what ignorance is"* (italics in original) (311). Thereby,
Hickman loved and nurtured the boy in order to vanquish his own bitterness and anger over the obliteration of his own family. We also know
that he dreamed that in this act of love, he would create an emissary,
someone Lincolnesque who could bridge the gap between black and
white, who could bring together politics and love. And though the transformation of Bliss to Sunraider is only hinted at, it is clear that the vehicle of this transformation is the spoken word, for Hickman recognizes his
own speaking techniques in use on the floor of the Senate when he is
vainly trying to warn Sunraider of the impending disaster that awaits
him. Sunraider even speculates as he lies dying with Hickman by his side
that the power of the preaching that Hickman taught him was somehow
too much for him: "What could I do with such power?" he asks. "I could
bring a big man to tears. I could topple him to his knees, make him shout,
crack him up with the ease with which shrill whistles split icebergs"
(112). But how he crosses the line from preaching love to practicing and
preaching the politics of hate, we never fully understand. And perhaps
Ellison himself never completely made this connection.

Still, we do understand the power of the black sermon. If Sunraider's
speech on the floor of the Senate is an exercise in absurdity, rhetoric at
its worst, the sermons that he remembers and in part recites as he lies
dying beside Hickman are an exploration of the other pole of rhetoric—
language as a touchstone for truth, language as incantation, propelling
the hearer beyond mere logic into a sublime sense of brotherhood, sister-
hood, freedom—thus John Callahan's well-chosen title for the novel,
Juneteenth, the day of freedom and atonement. In the introduction to
Juneteenth, Callahan recalls James Allan McPherson's response to hearing Ellison read in 1969 from what is now *Juneteenth*. After brooding for
years on what he had heard, he concluded that Ellison was doing more
than writing a novel. He was attempting to create a new form, a form
"invested with enough familiarity to reinvent a much broader and much

more diverse world for those who take their provisional identities from groups."[26] If McPherson was right, then once again we must wonder what the novel might have been had it been published in some sort of final form. We must also wonder if it might not have elaborated on the issues of speech that Ellison explores in *Invisible Man*. Is Sunraider's speech on the floor of the Senate the ultimate embodiment of political rhetoric, far, far more sinister than the "scientific" speech method that Ellison's invisible man was forced to learn by the Brotherhood? Are the sermons in *Juneteenth* the actual source of the speech techniques that Ellison's invisible man seems drawn to in front of the audiences he faces as a Brotherhood spokesperson? Once again, these questions can be answered only as far as a posthumous narrative will allow—with reservations.

The sermons that Bliss remembers are distillations of African-American rhetoric. They do not conform to the pattern that we explored for the traditional sermon in chapter one, an exercise in bringing life to a preordained text. Instead, they embody the sermon as liberation and improvisation, the sermons that Dolan Hubbard describes in his book *The Sermon and the African American Literary Imagination*. They are communal explorations of what happens when the text, or "the Word" as Hickman calls it, is improvised upon by a community of people. Dialogically, Bliss and Hickman explore the sermons they preached by remembering, reexamining them, and reproclaiming them. In so doing, they produce a new account of world history and American history. The first of these takes place in chapter six when Bliss/Sunraider, at Hickman's insistence and prodding, recites a sermon that he delivered based upon a sermon he had heard preached by the inimitable John P. Eatmore. Herein we discover a new account of creation that combines Hebrew traditions of human pride with Greek traditions of Prometheus the fire stealer. According to this version of human creation, after he is created and living among dinosaurs, man asks God for fire, but discovers only when God grants his prayer that he cannot handle fire. As God pours forth lava upon all of creation, everything cooks and man can only run in terror, unaware of the food that the fire has created, unaware also that he should have asked for wood so that he could make fire, not for fire itself. In evaluating man God says in a curious mixture of Old Testament rhetoric and down-home street talk, "My work is good; man knows now that he can't handle unleashed hell without suffering self-destruction! The time will come to pass when he shall forget it, but now I will give him a few billion years to grow, to shape his hand with toil, ... Yes, it will take him a few billion years before he'll discover pork chops and perhaps two more for fried chicken" (107). The combination of truth and humor here is strange to the mind accustomed to the traditional pattern of the sermon. It would seem that Eatmore's sermon, improvised upon by Bliss/Sunraider, is little more than a joke, but nothing could be further from the truth. As Hickman says, "He [Eatmore] knew the fundamental fact, that you must speak to the gut as well as to the heart and brain" (109).[27] Clearly, we as readers have reached the opposite pole of the scientific approach to speech that the Brotherhood called for in *Invisible Man*.

Furthermore, Bliss is describing the very process of transformation that has resulted in his own assassination. In becoming Sunraider, he has insisted upon fire—quite literally raided the sun—and he and those like him have brought down hell upon themselves as the end of the novel will imply. Man has been given the chance to learn, the chance to start again in America, but once again he has insisted upon fire instead of wood. All the while the very burning itself has produced food. A culture of people have survived the fire without succumbing to bitterness or vengeance. In their survival they have discovered the nourishment that suffering provides. These are the people whom Hickman represents, the people to whom the novel is dedicated: "That Vanished Tribe into Which I Was Born: The American Negro."

Significantly, after remembering and reproclaiming the Eatmore sermon, Bliss/Sunraider seeks to re-create the Juneteenth sermon, saying to Hickman, "Get back to that; back to a bunch of old fashioned Negroes celebrating an illusion of emancipation, and getting it all messed up with the Resurrection, minstrel shows, and vaudeville routines" (116). Sunraider does not recite this sermon so much as he re-creates it in his memory. Furthermore, the dialogic nature of this sermon is not a matter of Hickman and Bliss/Sunraider trading memories; rather it is a part of the form. The sermon was preached in call and response form. Hickman plays the role of Caller and Teacher—elder member of the group. Bliss plays the role of Responder and Student—learning the history of his race and nation. Once again we see Ellison using the form of the black sermon, not the white sermon. In short, the text is not proclaimed; it is discovered and improvised upon in a back-and-forth fashion. Once again we see the mingling of Greek and Hebrew cultures as well as the mingling of humor and seriousness. Much like the Hebrew God, the God that Hickman refers to has purpose and meaning in what he does. He is in charge of history. Thus, Africans are enslaved as an act of God, a way of

God giving them the Word. But in fulfilling God's will, the white man has acted in a "cruel, ungodly" manner. Their crime was such that Hickman compares it to the fall of Lucifer from Paradise. Like Lucifer, the white man went back on principles: "Because, Rev. Bliss, this was a country dedicated to the principles of Almighty God" (120). Yet in destroying African slaves and leaving them with nothing, in tearing them into small pieces, white Americans were "like a dope-fiend farmer planting a field with dragon teeth" (122). If we project the sermon onto the present tense of the scene at hand, the dragon teeth men who grow from these seeds are those who Sunraider dreams will drive him away at the end of the novel in the "Joe Cah."[28] Severen, the seed of Sunraider's loins, is also a progeny of dragon teeth, for he kills the man whose blood flows in his veins.

More interesting, however, than the theology or the history of the sermon that Bliss/Sunraider remembers is its form. The improvisational language of the minister actually becomes more of a factor in transforming and freeing the audience than the information or what we might call the text. When Hickman begins to enumerate what the enslavers took from African slaves and their descendents, Bliss responds with a catalog, epic in proportion but strangely mixing both humor and seriousness, much as the fried chicken and pork chops in the fire of the creation story in the Eatmore sermon: "Amen! And God—Count it, Rev. Bliss" (125) calls Hickman. Bliss responds, "Left eyeless, earless, noseless, throatless, teethless, toungueless, handless, feetless, armless, wrongless, rightless, harmless, drumless, songless, hornless, soundless, sightless, wrongless, rightless, motherless, fatherless, sisterless, brotherless, plowless muleless, foodless, mindless"(125). Bliss ends his catalog with "—and Godless, Rev. Hickman, did you say Godless?" (125). Hickman then responds by forging a metaphor that enables him to tie his own text to the Book of Ezekiel from the Old Testament. Hickman states: "And as we moldered underground, we were mixed with this land. We liked it. It fitted us fine. It was in us and we were in it" (125). Bliss's response a few lines later takes us to "the Word." As Hickman calls, "Give us a word" (125), Bliss responds with "the Word," pulling his language directly from the Book of Ezekiel: "WE WERE LIKE THE VALLEY OF DRY BONES!" (125). Hickman has now linked African-American history to Hebrew history, African-American culture to American soil, and African-American language to both American language as well as Hebrew language translated into English in the King James Bible. The preaching in this passage intermingles humor and seriousness, the Old Testament text, and homespun metaphors of folk culture. It forces the audience to recognize its own history in the Old Testament text. And yet it also forces the Old Testament text into a new form—one that is black and white, young and old, funny as well as serious, "multivoiced" as well as dialogic. When Hickman states a few passages later, "We had to take the Word for bread and meat," we recognize that he is doing more than using a metaphor. He is explaining the way in which the black church has enabled its legions of congregants to survive. It has enabled them to speak of their suffering, to speak of their pain, and to celebrate their joy. They have eaten of the fried chicken and the pork chops found in the wake of God's fire. The Word as proclaimed and recited and improvised upon is the recompense for the fire of slavery that burned all in its path.

Sunraider silences his memory of the Juneteenth sermon, thinking, *"No, ..., no more of it! No!"* (italics in original) (131). But Hickman, still at his bedside, begins recalling the event, retelling the story, making the novel we are reading every bit as dialogic as the sermons it describes. Once again, Hickman and Bliss/Sunraider are together reconstructing the events, re-proclaiming what has been proclaimed. Hickman recalls a veritable cornucopia of preaching with seven of the most accomplished ministers that Hickman knew anywhere, each trying to outdo the other. The minister whom Hickman refers to as "that little Negro Murray" preached the "pure Greek" and the "original Hebrew" in such a way that even the unlettered could understand, knowing "that oftentimes the meaning of the Word is in the way you make it sound" (137). And Hickman himself, trying to live up to the challenge set forth by Eatmore, sought what he calls "the Word within the Word that was both song and scream and whisper" (139). It is clear at this point that the preaching or the language that Hickman describes has moved beyond the logical correspondence between word and meaning into a realm of true transcendence, a kind of incantation. Hickman remembers that the Word was "so loud that it was silent, and so silent that it rang like a timeless gong" (139). He also remembers that in the transcendent state produced by the language, there was a recognition and an acceptance of what the church would normally define as evil: "Sure there was whiskey—and fornicating too. Always . . . , and just as Christ Jesus had to die between two criminals, just so did we have to put up with the whiskey and the fornication" (139). Hickman even recognizes the role that pride played in his own exalted use of language: "True there was preacher pride in it, there always is" (139). What he cannot recognize perhaps is that if the rhetoric of the Word can produce joy, can be food for those who converge to hear, it can also be used to create hate and divisiveness. Bliss/Sunraider was indeed struck with the power of the Word; but when he began to explore the limits of his power, he found that there was more than preacher pride in it. He found the fire of plain old human pride, the very force that, according to Hickman, brought Lucifer hurtling down into hell.

In such a context, it is appropriate then that Ellison's novel should end with a vision of hell, a hell created by rhetoric. As Sunraider goes in and out of consciousness during what we imagine must be the last moments of his life, he hears and then fails to hear the voice of Hickman beside him. Like the father he has always been, Hickman calls to his adopted son in these words: "Son, are you there?" (321). But finally, when the voice fades, Sunraider's mind is filled no longer with the sermons of old, but with surreal dreams, the last of which ends the novel and ties together the speech on the Senate floor with one of the central themes of the novel—the ability of African Americans to improvise.

The senator dreams that in crossing a boulevard, he is followed by a long black car. When the three occupants of the car disembark, looking much like the hipsters in the last chapters of *Invisible Man*, one asks him "how's this for a goongauge?" The senator soon realizes, "This was no Cadillac, no Lincoln, Oldsmobile or Buick. . .; it was an arbitrary assemblage of chassis, wheels, engine, hood horns, none of which had ever been part of a single car. It was a junkyard sculpture mechanized! An improvisation, a bastard creation of black bastards" (347). Thus, the Sunraider must confront his failure of insight. In his speech on the Senate floor (the last speech of his life, we must assume) he has failed to understand the true nature of improvisation. He assumes that African-American use of the Cadillac is merely the misappropriation of the Cadillac, the ultimate American symbol of wealth and power. But the "Joe Cah" shows that true improvisation redefines the whole notion of what a car is. His other failure is one of pride. In using the power of rhetoric (learned in the sermons of old) to create hate and division, he has misappropriated "the Word" and thereby created a host of enemies but nothing truly original. He has asked for fire and not for wood. Three of these enemies, dragon teeth progeny, have used words to make their own motto. They plan to ride him to hell in the Joe Cah, a word that improvises upon the more familiar word "joker." Sounding very much like Ras the Destroyer, one of the three unnamed black men tells Sunraider, "remembah us mah-toe, mahn: Down Wid de Coon Cawdge/Up .WID DE JOE CAH!" They ultimately plan to "KICK HIM ASS," but before that "we give his butt a little ride" (348). As a dark hand reaches down for the senator, he hears the "consoling voice" of Hickman calling from above him. But we must come to the conclusion finally that Hickman cannot help him now. The funeral carriage has arrived, and he will be carried to hell in the very vehicle he has brought into being with his misuse of the Word. The Joe Cah was brought into being in an effort to do away with the Cooncage Eight. It is the ultimate *joke* upon the senator. Thus, Ellison's novel ends, mixing humor and horror into a deadly serious portrayal of American culture and American politics. More than simply a portrayal of a rhetorical hell, John Callahan sees in this surreal ending "Ellison's intimation through Sunraider's delirious consciousness, of the coming of the Black Power movement."[29]

In such an observation, we again see the surprising scope of this book. Though conceived and set in the fifties, Ellison's novel continued to evolve as he worked on it, drawing in finally both the Civil Rights movement and the Black Power movement. Sunraider misappropriates the voice of the black sermon into the race-baiting political rhetoric that we encounter on the first pages of the novel, but at the end of his life, he is privileged to see his own misappropriated rhetoric transformed yet again into something that he cannot explain. One cannot help but wonder if thereby Ellison's vision captured the bloodshot eyes of many white Americans who stood passively by and watched as passive resistance was replaced with active rebellion.

For all of his power with the Word, Hickman is finally like Ellison's invisible man, another man intrigued with the power of language: he cannot help anyone in the end. His grand experiment failed, he can only watch as the Word is perverted just as Plato long ago feared that it would be. With the senator dying, he can console the one, but the many (at least those outside of his own congregation) are left to go their own way. Much like the audience at Tod Clifton's funeral, they are leaderless. Like the Fool in Shakespeare's *King Lear*, Hickman is empowered to see the turmoil all around him, even to describe it in unforgettable language, but he is powerless to do anything about it. And just as Ellison's invisible man is left forever in his unfinished hibernation, so Alonzo Hickman is frozen at the bedside of the one man who he had hoped might help. He calls again, but in the end, no one responds.

As we place these two figures together, it is tempting to assume too much, to assume that the symmetry I have just noted was planned, that Ellison ardently sought such an ending. But once again we must remember that this is a part of an extended posthumous novel and that the ending Ellison planned was perhaps never finished in any final form. What we have is finally a kind of Joe Cah, an amazing combination of parts, creating something totally new in the history of literature, leading toward an unknown end. Still, we can assume that in what we have of his last work, Ellison did achieve some remarkable feats. He explored and extended the art of the African-American sermon, creating and re-creating and improvising upon the form. What we have of the novel itself suggests that it might indeed have been a new type of novel, one that, as McPherson seemed to sense, merged the African-American sermon and the novel. Still, the one feat that Ellison did not achieve in this novel is what he seemed to promise in his speech for the National Book Award, namely, a fully achieved attempt at a major novel. The other is the one that his invisible man sought vainly at the funeral of Tod Clifton, namely, a mixing of politics and love.

Notes

1. William Gibson, "Introduction," in Mark Twain, *The Mysterious Stranger,* ed. William Gibson (Berkeley: University of California Press, 1970), 2.

2. Ibid.

3. Christopher C. De Santis, "'Some cord of kinship stronger and deeper than blood': An Interview with John F. Callahan, Editor of Ralph Ellison's *Juneteenth,*" *African American Review* 34 (2000): 610. In the "Afterword: A Note to Scholars" which is appended to the published version of *Juneteenth,* Callahan phrases this in a slightly different manner: "As I tried to discern one coherent, inclusive sequence, I realized slowly, somewhat against my will, that although Ellison had hoped to write one big book, his saga, like William Faulkner's, would not be contained with in the pages of a single novel." John Callahan, "Afterword: A Note to Scholars," in Ralph Ellison, *Juneteenth,* ed. John Callahan (New York: Vintage, 1999), 23.

4. John Callahan, "Introduction" in *Juneteenth* (New York: Vintage, 1999), xxii.

5. John Callahan, Phone conversation with the author, 8 May 2003.

6. John Callahan, "Afterword: A Note to Scholars," in Ralph Ellison, *Juneteenth* ed. John Callahan (New York: Vintage, 1999), 365.

7. Christopher C. De Santis, "'Some cord of kinship' . . .: An Interview with John F. Callahan, Editor of Ralph Ellison's *Juneteenth,*" 612.

8. I attempted to interview Mrs. Ellison on this matter. She very politely declined my request for an interview through her lawyer, directing me to contact Professor Callahan.

9. John Callahan, Phone conversation with the author, 8 May 2003.

10. Avon Kirkland, "Ralph Ellison," *American Masters*, PBS, February 21, 2002.

11. Ibid.

12. John Callahan, "Introduction," xxi.

13. Ibid.

14. John Hersey, "A Completion of Personality: A Talk with Ralph Ellison," TCERE, 791.

15. Ibid.

16. Ibid, 793.

17. John Callahan, Phone conversation with the author, 8 May 2003.

18. Professor Callahan includes only some of the "literally thousands" (Callahan, "Afterword: A Note to Scholars," 351) of notes that Ellison took on the novel, listing those that he found illuminating. One must wonder, however, which notes he did not include. Once again the critic is left with Callahan's judgment on this matter. Due to his work on the scholarly edition of *Juneteenth,* the material concerning the second novel at the Library of Congress are not open to scholars. When Professor Callahan publishes the scholarly edition of *Juneteenth*, all files at the Library of Congress will be open to other scholars (Callahan, "Afterword: A Note to Scholars," 368).

19. Ibid., 352.

20. Ibid., 357.

21. Ibid., 360.

22. Ibid., 353.

23. Hickman thinks during Sunraider's speech, "Ah but the glory of that baby boy. I could never forget it." Ralph Ellison, *Juneteenth* (New York: Vintage, 1999), 36. All subsequent references to the text of *Juneteenth* will be followed by the page number of quotation cited in text in parenthesis. In cases where the context does not make clear to which of Ellison's novels I am referring, I will place the abbreviation *J* before the page number.

24. The reader will remember no doubt that Hickman has received word that Sunraider will be assassinated. Ellison's notes make clear the fact that Sunraider is in fact being shot by the son he has denied, the person whom Hickman calls Severen after the moment of the assassination. Ellison's note on this matter reads as follows: "Thus his denial of Severen and his refusal to see him or to accept his role of father. (The old American refusal to recognize its racial diversity.)" (359).

25. In fact, John Callahan has advanced this argument on a slightly different front, stating: "At the end of *Invisible Man,* the narrator asks the question, 'Who knows but that, on the lower frequencies, I speak for you?' Ellison proceeds to

pick up Invisible Man's challenge in *Juneteenth*. The latter is a multi-layered narrative, multi-focused, multi-voiced, and multi-toned." In short, Ellison does indeed speak for all of America. Christopher C. De Santis, "Some Cord of Kinship," 607.

26. Callahan, "Introduction," *xxix*.

27. Hickman clarifies and expands this point later when discussing the Juneteenth sermon: "I'm not just talking about the eating. I mean the communion, the coming together—of which the eating was only a part; an outward manifestation, a symbol, like the Blood is signified by wine, and the Flesh by the bread " (133).

28. Those who drive Sunraider away at the end of the novel are poignantly aware of his sins, in particular his proposal of a new name for the Cadillac:

And remembah us mah-toe, mahn
　　Down wid de Coon Cawdge
　　Up WID DE JOE CAH! (348)

29. John Callahan, letter to the author, 2 June 2003.

Conclusion

"The American novel is . . . a conquest of the frontier; as it describes our experience, it creates it."
—Ralph Ellison, "The Art of Fiction: An Interview"

In an 1851 letter to Nathaniel Hawthorne, written during the torturous
last months of his seventeen-month struggle with *Moby Dick*, a thirty-
one-year-old Herman Melville described the dilemma he faced in completing what he hoped might be his masterpiece: "What I feel most
moved to write, that is banned,—it will not pay. Yet, altogether, write the
other way I cannot. So the product is a final hash, and all my books are
botches."[1] Looking back at this letter from the vantage point of the
twenty-first century gives us an interesting perspective on the American
novel. Melville had come onto the American scene as a writer of adventure stories about the sea. He wrote these stories out of his own experiences as a sailor and in the process amassed quite a readership. But as he
evolved as a writer into more serious novels about the sea, as he began to
delve into metaphysics in his fiction, he found to his dismay that his audience left him. *Moby Dick* indeed became not the culmination of Melville's career as a writer, but the death knell. Described as a *writ de lunatico* by one reviewer,[2] the novel effectively ended Melville's ability to
sell books though he continued heroically to write them. Ironically, the
same novel became the very book that revived Melville's career some
twenty or so years after his death. In fact, modern readers have encountered the plot of *Moby Dick* in every form imaginable, even cartoon
form. No canon of nineteenth-century American literature would be

complete without *Moby Dick.* Some novel theorists have even gone so far as to call it the best novel we have.[3]

Still, many American writers who followed him might well have understood Melville's frustration as well as his experience subsequent to the letter to Hawthorne. For though pursuing a great "whale" of a novel (as Melville called *Moby Dick)* might make a writer valuable to posterity, such a pursuit might not enrich a writer or make him popular in his lifetime. Melville felt keenly the sting of his lost reputation as well as the penury that loss brought. He complained to Hawthorne in that same letter, "Dollars damn me,"[4] and after the failure of *Moby Dick* he was to discover even more poverty than he had found before it. As he pursued his great whale, his personal damnation was in some sense final.

As his essays demonstrate, Ellison was a great admirer of nineteenth-century American fiction. He saw Melville's *Moby Dick* and Mark Twain's *Huckleberry Finn* as "our two great nineteenth-century novels."[5] Still, as a novelist, Ellison was quite different in his aspirations than either Melville or Twain. Twain managed to write profound novels and make money at the same time.[6] Melville dreamed of combining money and craft, and as we see in the letter to Hawthorne, he was sorely disappointed when he learned that it could not be done. He even implied in his letter to Hawthorne that he botched his books in an effort to make them both profitable and worthy of the name novel. Ellison seems never to have considered money to be an object of aspiration even close in importance to the development of craft. In a long, whimsical letter to Saul Bellow dated May 4, 1956, Ellison writes: "To hell with those bastards who think writing is done to keep the pockets of their Brooks Brothers Grey Flannel suits stuffed with dollars, we know that its [sic] the ride of the narrative and the all too infrequent rising flights into poetry that we live for."[7] In a March 18, 1959, letter to Bellow, Ellison thanks his friend for securing him a lecture at Middlebury College: "I was in great need of dough."[8] Similarly in his letters to Albert Murray during this time period and later, he complains of not having money for the luxury items he wants (stereos, cameras), but he does not ever project onto the future a novel that will bring him the money he wants. He makes his living as he can, lecturing extensively, living on his royalties from *Invisible Man* and his wife Fanny's salary. We may safely conclude then that securing his future or even increasing his income by finishing another novel must have been secondary to getting the second novel right.

Ellison's responses to attempts to buy the film rights for *Invisible Man* also support this conclusion. In a letter dated May 17, 1980, Ellison responds to Kimball Baker's request for film rights, a request that included a screenplay that Baker had written adapting *Invisible Man* for film. Ellison writes: "Since its publication in 1952, various writers, directors, composers, and producers—of professional and non-professional dimension—have expressed interest in adapting the novel to their preference. I have been consistent in my refusal because I prefer that the book rest on its merits as a novel to be read rather than transposed into a form for which it was not written."[9] Allowing the novel to be adapted for film would have been a relatively painless way of enriching himself, even of funding more time to work on the second novel, but as this letter indicates, Ellison never seriously considered such a move. His commitment to the craftsmanship of the novel was such that he could not agree to the changes in form that a film version of *Invisible Man* would entail. Ellison maintained this position until his death.

Lawrence Jackson writes in his biography of Ellison that the virtues that Ellison witnessed among the jazz musicians of Oklahoma City when he was growing up made them into "religious martyrs" for him.[10] Jackson uses "Living with Music," an essay from *Shadow and Act,* as a way of supporting this observation. Therein Ellison writes: "Their [the jazz musicians of Ellison's childhood] driving motivation was neither money nor fame, but the will to achieve the most eloquent expression of idea-emotions through the technical mastery of their instruments (which incidentally, some of them wore as a priest wears the cross)."[11] It is hard not to see a connection between these early models and Ellison's own career as a novelist. He wrote not for money and not for fame, but to create art. In this regard Ellison differs from Melville and Twain, both of whom backed into the process of writing great novels after finding fame and fortune in other types of writing—Twain by way of the travelogue and Melville by way of the adventure story. Ellison differs in this regard from his own nameless narrator of *Invisible Man* who, as I argued in chapters one and two, becomes a rabble-rouser for hire because the money is right. There is no Brotherhood urging Ellison to write. In short, Ellison became a writer of novels because he loved the craft in the same way that the musicians of his youth loved music. At another point in "Living with Music" Ellison might indeed be describing his own aspirations as he remembers the musicians of his youth: "Life could be harsh, loud and wrong if it wished, but they lived it fully, and when they expressed their attitude toward the world it was with a fluid style that reduced the chaos of living to form."[12] The form becomes for the musician the way of shaping life into a pattern just as to Ellison's invisible man form finally is the escape from chaos: "In going underground, I whipped it all except the mind, the *mind*. And the mind that has conceived a plan of living must never lose sight of the chaos against which that pattern was conceived" (580). But if the artist as priest or musician must find a form that serves as a bulwark against chaos, if Ellison's invisible man finds a pattern in the underground, what are we to make of Ellison's ultimate failure to finish the second novel? Was it a failure of form? Or was it a failure to complete the gesture that he began in *Invisible Man*, to find "a socially responsible role for an invisible man"? We return to questions that must ultimately be rhetorical, for even if Ellison were still with us, one doubts that he would know the answers. Still, we can safely make some assumptions about Ellison and perhaps that is the most we can hope for, given the ultimate invisibility that Ellison's invisible man sees at the core of human nature.

The forms Ellison explores in *Juneteenth* were clearly different from any type of fictional forms that had ever been created in American literature. Ellison suggested in "The World and the Jug" that Hemingway arrived at something like blues, which was as close as Americans had come to the true spirit of tragedy. Perhaps in *Juneteenth* Ellison aspires to a similar merging of forms: the call-and-response sermon pattern permeates and ultimately determines the form of the novel. It even becomes the source for the political speech we hear Sunraider deliver on the floor of the Senate. But more important, in *Juneteenth* the humor and seriousness of the black sermon reach the level of the sublime. Hickman dares to hope that his rhetoric might ultimately reach the level of the Gettysburg Address as he fantasizes that Bliss will become another Lincoln, that he will take the words forged in the black church all the way to Washington and bring about a new day for the oppressed. That these forms can only become a part of American culture in their bastardized embodiment as the words of the race-baiting Senator Sunraider is the unique tragedy of the novel. Yet when we put the novel into the context of history, we find a central irony: while Ellison toiled away on his second novel, a black minister went to Washington and uttered those famous words from the Old Testament, what Dolan Hubbard calls "the most responsive mascon in the peculiar eschatology of the black church": "Let my people go."[13] And though his most famous utterance of these words was not to take place until 1963, the storm clouds were forming in the fifties in cities such as Montgomery, Little Rock, Albany, and Jackson—across the entire Southland. Even as Ellison conceived of the incidents and characters that would form the core of what we now know as

Juneteenth, the political gestures that he dreamed of in fiction were being expressed in reality, were becoming parts of history. And one must wonder what effect this had on Ellison's progress on the second novel, on the vision of an American novel that brought together the "many strands" that Ellison's invisible man sees in American culture at the end of *Invisible Man*.

John Callahan stated to me that the manuscript of the so-called second novel indicates that Ellison continued to work on what is now *Juneteenth* until 1986.[14] Callahan states in "The Making of *Juneteenth*" that Ellison began working with the central characters in *Juneteenth* in the fifties.[15] His letters during that period seem to indicate that he initially planned to finish the novel while still in Rome. In that same May 4 letter to Bellow quoted above, Ellison describes applying for a second year of his fellowship there in order to finish the novel. Having been sick with pneumonia, he did not get as much work done on the book as he had hoped: "after the sickness I got panicy [sic] and asked for a second year and I'm told I am likely to get it. I just couldn't face the possibility of stopping my work and packing to come home. I hope we can stay, especially if the book isn't finished by Oct."[16] Had Ellison followed this implied timeline, the book would have been finished in October 1956 or sometime in 1957. The publication would have occurred sometime in 1958. Two years later in March 1959, Ellison still had not finished the book. He was living in Saul Bellow's house at Tivoli in Minnesota and again trying to finish the novel. He wrote to Bellow: "What I'd like to do is finish the first draft by August then [sic] see what kind of advance my publishers would be willing to lay out while I worked it into final shape."[17] Did the early events of the Civil Rights movement modify this plan or was it simply a matter of what Ellison described in a March 1957 letter to Granville Hicks concerning his essay for *The Living Novel* as "that mysterious darkness which we call writer's block"?[18] Was the failure to finish or publish the novel some odd combination of these forces, a world that was already beginning to change Ellison's conception of the Civil Rights movement, perhaps of Alonzo Hickman and Bliss and the "mysterious darkness" that all writers face? We again come face to face with a question that will probably never be answered. Nonetheless, something important and decisive must have happened since the novel was not delayed a year or two years or even five years, but for the rest of Ellison's life, some thirty-five years.

If the debates of the late fifties and early sixties steadily transformed Ellison's conception of the emerging manuscript, one can only imagine how the public debate of later dates might have impacted his attempts to finalize the novel. Not only did the Civil Rights movement itself redefine the discussion of race in this country but also the movement itself fostered other more radical movements. Malcolm X became the foil for Martin Luther King, Jr., advocating, "whatever means necessary" to create a more equitable country, advocating not integration but separatism. Ellison's letters to Albert Murray and others as well as his public statements on the matter indicate that Ellison favored integration and backed the Civil Rights movement. But the whole notion of separatism, espoused by Malcolm X and later the Black Power movement, ran counter to Ellison's thinking. Ellison's fiction clearly demonstrates the strength of diversity that his invisible man refers to in the epilogue to *Invisible Man* when he says, "Whence all this passion toward conformity anyway?—diversity is the word. . . . America is woven of many strands" (577). As Robert O'Meally pointed out in a recent documentary, even late in his career, Ellison's vision of America was very much that of a diverse population that would come to recognize and confront the consequences of diversity. O'Meally recalls Ellison speaking at Harvard and pointedly challenging the audience to consider how every white member of the audience was in some ways black and every black member of the audience was in some ways white.[19] The vision expressed here is very much the vision that is expressed in *Juneteenth,* a world where black and white come together not only on the level of equality under the law but also on the level of art. In this context, *Juneteenth* is a novel that insists upon recognition: the black knowing and being the white and the white knowing and being the black.

Still, as time passed, did the difficulties of publishing such a novel become apparent to Ellison or did current events continue to transform the work itself? In a speech given in 1969, Amiri Baraka (Leroi Jones), one of Ellison's most vocal critics, essentially defined the nature of black art in such a way that Ellison could not be a black artist unless he was a Black nationalist: "The Negro artist who is not a nationalist at this late date is a white artist, even without knowing it. He is creating death snacks, for and out of dead stuff."[20] The Black Arts movement, of which Baraka was a spokesperson, made Ellison and his work into an archetype for the proverbial Uncle Tom. And though there is no direct evidence to suggest that this movement or any other kept Ellison from finishing or publishing his second novel or any subsequent work, one wonders if it did not at the very least begin to transform his conception of the characters and incidents that make up *Juneteenth.* Ironically, Ellison once again found himself in a situation similar to the one he had been forced into by Irving Howe's "Black Boys and Native Sons" in 1963. Ellison's interpretation of his own experience was called into question.

The whole process of defining rigidly what black art is, of distinguishing black art from white art, runs in direct opposition to the vision that Ellison's 1952 novel sets forth. As Ellison stated in an undated letter to Saul Bellow, his main perception in *Invisible Man* was: "That when the individual is willing to make an effort to free himself from illusions of the socalled [sic] race problem he discovers the gateway to possibility. No outsider can make him free, he must win his freedom, his sense of possibility."[21] Later in this same letter, Ellison complains that it is not the narrowness of black life that he notices, but its breadth: "It is not that I rush toward my identity as a Negro—why rush toward something which one can only recognize as inevitable?—I simply recognize that problems [sic] simply another form of the human predicament."[22] Being black is a part of the larger reality of being human. Within the novel, the struggle then is not to define color but to define humanity in all of its color and diversity. In that way, one takes "personal moral responsibility for democracy."[23] In that way, one finds the connection between the one and the many.

Baraka's implied definition of Ellison's and other non-nationalists' work as "death snacks" by default can only be like the Brotherhood's scientific approach to history—an attempt to confine and contain that which is essentially beyond complete definition or control. It can only be like Senator's Sunraider's definition of the Cadillac as the Cooncage Eight: an attempt to make an American icon ethnically pure. Indeed, the novelist who submits to such a rigid definition of his or her work would be running counter to the freedom implicit in the form of the novel itself, what Bakhtin calls the "anticanonical" quality of the novel. Such a novelist would also be surrendering what to Ellison was the core of the novel—the freedom to use one's experience, whatever that experience may be, and thereby to shape the experience of democracy. In short, the very argument that Ellison used to answer Irving Howe in "The World and the Jug" might be used to refute Baraka: refusing the writer the ability to define his experience as broadly as possible denies him or her the freedom to write. It diminishes what for Ellison stood at the core of all novels, namely, the breadth and complexity of the human condition.

Placed in this context, Ellison's struggle becomes much more than just one man's struggle with one book. It is a struggle with the novel itself and the whole idea of black men and women and white men and women and Asian and Hispanic men and women and Native American men and women writing American novels. The first writers of African-American literature wrote within the context of a kind of straight-jacket of the slave narrative, as John Sekora has pointed out.[24] The slave narrative was the story of a slave written to demonstrate that the slave could write, to demonstrate that slavery dehumanized, but not to express the particularity of human experience. But as Henry Louis Gates has pointed out, the twentieth century thrust the African-American writer into a new struggle, a struggle with form.[25] Black literacy was a fact; for the twentieth century the question would be what form the black writer would choose when he or she wrote. Would he or she write about black themes using white forms as Countee Cullen did? Or would there be new forms, forms such as that which Zora Neale Hurston discovers in *Their Eyes Were Watching God,* a form that Gates calls in *The Signifying Monkey* "the speakerly text."[26] Ellison took that struggle one step further. He asked a question that has still not been answered: what form will the American novel itself take? What will it look like when American writers and readers stop asking about the ethnicity of the writer and start discovering the way in which that ethnicity has brought into being a form that is woven of many strands, a form without specific color or ethnicity, a form that is truly American. It was a big question that we are still answering. And since it is so big, perhaps we can forgive Ellison's failure to finish that "fully achieved attempt at a major novel" that he had implicitly promised in 1952.[27] After all, his persistence and consistency in asking the question again and again took profound courage.

Still, after acknowledging all that we owe Ellison for his courage and his insight, we must return to a question that stands at the heart of the novel itself and the heart of this study: that of history. Ellison recognized the relationship between the novel and history; otherwise, he would never have even considered it important for the novelist to take responsibility for democracy. Otherwise, he would have never been so successful at capturing the texture of black life and black history in *Invisible Man.* And yet despite his attempt to be responsible for democracy, Ellison ultimately failed as so many other American writers have done. As good a historian as he was, Ellison did not in his hibernating invisible man account for Martin Luther King, Jr., or Malcolm X or the bizarre chaos of events that made Birmingham into Bombingham and haphazardly photographed passersby like Walter Gadsden into unnamed cultural icons. The slow, frozen wheels of justice began to turn, and chance and rhetoric seemed to play equal parts in opening the bloodshot eyes of a nation whose citizens, as Ellison had predicted, would prefer to look the other way.

Ironically, perhaps in his very failure Ellison was once again a quintessentially American writer. Emily Budick asserts in *Fiction and Historical Consciousness: The American Romance Tradition* that American writers have an ambiguous relationship to history. They insist upon setting their stories in a recognizable historical landscape, but their characters are forever imprisoned in their own subjective views of the history that surrounds them.[28] History serves in this context to remind the writer as well as the reader of what Frederick Jameson describes in *The Political Unconscious* as the ultimate horizon of events, that which must finally frame all of our fictions and all of our art and all of our dreams. Thus, Ellison, like the writers he admired—Hawthorne and Melville and Faulkner and Hemingway, and countless others—never quite captured the mystery of race or of justice in America. But like them, in his failure he created a world that forever changed us all.

Notes

1. Herman Melville, Letter to Nathaniel Hawthorne, in *Moby–Dick A Norton Critical Edition,* Ed. Harrison Hayford and Hershel Parker (New York: Norton, 1967), 558.

2. Anonymous, "[Cause for a Writ *de Lunatico*]," in *Moby–Dick A Norton Critical Edition,* Ed. Harrison Hayford and Hershel Parker (New York: Norton, 1967), 558.

3. Andrew Delbanco, "Introduction," Herman Melville, *Moby-Dick or The Whale* (New York: Penguin, 1992), xi.

4. Herman Melville, Letter to Nathaniel Hawthorne, 557.

5. Ralph Ellison, "The Art of Fiction: An Interview," *TCERE*, 223.

6. Twain did, however, go bankrupt in the 1890s after several of his business ventures succumbed during the Panic of 1891.

7. REM, LOC, box 37, folder 7.

8. Ibid.

9. REM, LOC, box 153, folder 4.

10. Lawrence Jackson, *Ralph Ellison: Emergence of Genius* (New York: John Wiley and Sons, 2002), 67.

11. Ralph Ellison, "Living With Music," *TCERE*, 229.

12. Ibid.

13. Dolan Hubbard, *The Sermon and the African-American Literary Imagination* (Columbia: University of Missouri Press, 1994), 83.

14. John Callahan, Phone conversation with the author, 8 May 2003.

15. John Callahan, "The Making of Juneteenth" *Columbia: A Journal of Literature and Art* 36 (2002): 180.

16. REM, LOC, box 37, folder 7.

17. REM, LOC, box 37, folder 7. Though it is impossible to gauge just what prevented Ellison from finishing his novel, it is clear that he struggled with it during the late fifties and early sixties, always hoping to get the book out. On January 19, 1960, Ellison writes to Bellow, "I haven't been able to work for two weeks and I feel that I'm falling apart. I find myself in strange places in my dreams and during the days Hickman and Bliss and Severen seem like people out of some faded dream of nobility. They need desperately to be affirmed while I seem incapable of bringing them to full life." REM, LOC, box 37, folder 7.

18. REM, LOC, box 106, folder 8.

19. Avon Kirkland, "Ralph Ellison," *American Masters*, PBS, February 21, 2002.

20. Imamu Amiri Baraka, *Raise, Race, Rays, Raze: Essays since 1965* (New York: Random House, 1971), 98.

21. REM, LOC, box 37, folder 7.

22. Ibid.

23. Ralph Ellison, "Brave Words for a Startling Occasion," TCERE, 151.

24. John Sekora, "Comprehending Slavery: Language and Personal History in the *Narrative*," in *Modern Critical Interpretations: Narrative of the Life of Frederick Douglass*, Ed. Harold Bloom (New York: Chelsea House, 1988), 154.

25. Henry Louis Gates, Jr., *Figures in Black: Words, Signs, and the Racial Self* (Oxford: Oxford University Press, 1987), 4.

26. Henry Louis Gates, Jr., The *Signifying Monkey* (New York: Oxford University Press, 1988), 21-22.

27. Ralph Ellison, "Brave Words for a Startling Occasion," *TCERE*, 151.

28. Emily Budick, *Fiction and Historical Consciousness: the American Romance Tradition* (New Haven, Conn.: Yale University Press, 1989), 5.

Index

Abernathy, Ralph David, 93, 103

Abolitionist movement, 36, 39, 74

Absalom, Absalom! (novel by William Faulkner), 59

African nationalism, 8

African-American sermon, 17-19, 123-26, 128

anaphora, 99

Anatomy of Criticism (book by Northrop Frye), 61

anticanonical quality of the novel, 60, 62, 137

American Novel and Its Tradition, The (book by Richard Chase), 59

Antioch Review, 58

Aristotle, 18, 19, 61, 97

Armstrong, Louis, 3, 48, 51

Associated Press, 106

"Atlanta Exposition Address" (speech by Booker T. Washington), 26, 41, 101

Augustine, 16

Baker, Kimball, 135

Bakhtin, Mikhail, 59, 60, 62, 139

Baldwin, James, 72, 73

Baraka, Amiri (Leroi Jones), 136, 137

Barbee, Homer (character in *Invisible Man*), 8, 10, 15, 18, 40, 43, 48

Battle Royal (incident in *Invisible Man*), 8, 9, 10, 25, 26, 28, 29, 30, 31, 40, 43, 48, 68

Bearden, Romare, 57, 91

Bellow, Saul, 134-35, 139

Beloved (novel by Toni Morrison), 74

Bill of Rights, 65

Birmingham, 102-6, 109, 138

Black Arts movement, 138

"Black Boys and Native Sons" (essay by Irving Howe), 2, 71, 139

Black nationalism, 138

Black Power movement, 21, 45, 93-94, 119, 136

Bledsoe, Herbert A. (character in *Invisible Man*), 43

blues, 75, 77, 131, 135-36
Book of Ezekiel, 124
Branch, Taylor, 97-100, 105-6
Brilioth, Yngve, 16
Brockway, Lucious (character
    in *Invisible Man*), 8
Brother Jack (character in
    Invisible Man), 8, 11, 28,
    29, 30, 35-37, 40, 52, 101,
    131
Brotherhood (organization in
    Invisible Man), 8-11, 19, 29,
    30-31, 34-40, 42-46, 95, 98,
    101, 103-04, 123-24, 135,
    137
Budick, Emily, 141
Bunche, Ralph, 32-33
Burnett, Whit, 95
bus boycotts, 32, 93, 102,   117

Cadillac, 18, 113, 121, 127, 138
call and response, 10, 17, 28,
    30, 41, 95, 97-100,124-26,
    134
Call and Response (anthology
    edited by Patricia Liggins
    Hill), 37
Callahan, John, 2, 52, 71, 78,
    83, 114-17, 120-22, 128-31,
    137
Catcher in the Rye, The (book
    by J. D. Salinger), 59
Chase, Richard, 59-61
Children's Campaign, 104
Christianity, 19, 36, 117, 126
Civil Rights Bill, 106
Civil Rights movement, 2, 20,
    31, 52, 93-97, 102-7, 120,
    136-37
Civil War, 93, 107

Clifton, Tod (character in
    Invisible Man), 10, 25, 34,
    38-44, 46, 94-96, 98-101,
    104-5, 116, 128-29
Cold War, 15, 66
*Columbia History of the
    American Novel, The* (book
    by Emory Elliott), 60
Communist Party, 15, 32, 45
Confessions of Nat Turner, The
    (book by William Styron),
    109
Connor, Eugene "Bull," 103,
    105
Constitution, 33, 64-65, 67, 76,
    78, 120
contemporaneity as a quality of
    the novel, 61-63
Coon-Cage Eight (Sunraider's
    name for the Cadillac in
    Juneteenth), 18, 111, 113,
    121, 128
Crane, Stephen, 69
Cuban Missile Crisis, 66
Cullen, Countee, 140

Daughters of the American
    Revolution, 33
De Santis, Christopher, 114-15
Declaration of Independence,
    19, 64, 67, 78, 118
democracy, 4, 51, 64, 67, 68-69,
    71, 80-81, 91, 107, 109,
    119, 140-41
Derrida, Jacques, 14, 47
Descartes, Rene, 62
Dexter Avenue Baptist Church,
    98
dialogic quality of the novel, 62,
    123-24

Direction (periodical), 64
Dissent (periodical), 71
donnée, 70, 74
Dostoevsky, Fyodor, 75
Douglass, Frederick, 9, 35-39, 75
Du Bois, W. E. B., 32-33, 45

Eatmore, John P. (character in *Juneteenth*), 123
Eidothea, 67
Eliot, Thomas Sterns, 75, 79
Elliott, Emory, 60
Ellison, Fanny, 115, 117
Ellison, Ida, 14

Ellison, Ralph,
  Collections of Essays:
    Collected Essays of Ralph Ellison, The, 72, 131
    Going to the Territory, 14
    Shadow and Act, 14, 72, 79, 133
  Individual Essays:
    "Beating that Boy," 58
    "Charlie Christian Story, The," 82
    "Golden Age, Time Past," 82
    "Hidden Name and Complex Fate," 60, 71, 79, 80-81
    "Living With Music," 135
    "Novel as a Function of American Democracy, The," 1, 3, 81
    "On Bird, Bird Watching and Jazz," 82
    "Perspectives of Literature," 81

"Remembering Jimmy," 82
"Richard Wright and Negro Fiction," 64
"Society, Morality and the Novel," 25, 57, 63, 65, 70
"Stephen Crane and the Mainstream of American Fiction," 69
"Twentieth Century Fiction and the Black Mask of Humanity," 64, 66, 70
"World and the Jug, The," 57, 71-72, 75-79, 134, 137
Novels:
  Invisible Man, 1, 4, 7, 9, 11, 12, 14, 15, 18, 19, 20, 25-58, 62, 64-68, 72-73, 76, 78, 91, 93-99, 101, 103, 105-9, 114, 116, 118, 119-123, 125, 134-36, 137-140
  epilogue to *Invisible Man*, 8, 12, 20, 40, 44, 47, 49, 50, 78, 138
  prologue to *Invisible Man*, 9, 48, 96
  Invisible Man, adaptation to film, 134-35
  Juneteenth, 2, 3, 10, 14, 15, 18, 53, 64, 101, 111, 113-24, 136-39
  problems with the second novel, 1, 2, 52, 53, 58, 59, 68, 113, 114, 116, 134-38
Emancipation Proclamation, 107, 109, 117
Emerson, Ralph Waldo, 8, 14
"Epic and Novel" (essay by Mikhail Bakhtin), 59

"Everybody's Protest Novel"
    (essay by James Baldwin),
    72

Faulkner, William, 59, 63, 65,
    75, 141
Foley, Barbara, 15, 50
Founder, The (character in
    Invisible Man), 29, 43
Frye, Northrop, 59, 61-62

Gadsden, Walter, 106-7, 109,
    141
Garvey, Marcus, 45-46
Gates, Henry Louis, 140
Gettysburg Address, 136
Golden Day (bar in *Invisisible
    Man*), 8
Greek culture, 60, 123-26, 125
Green Hills of Africa (book by
    Ernest Hemingway), 79
Gumbel, Bryant, 115

Hambro (character in *Invisible
    Man*), 34
Hawthorne, Nathaniel, 60-61,
    70, 81, 133-34, 141
Hebrew culture, 123-26
Hemingway, Ernest, 75-79, 80-
    81, 136, 141
*Heroism and the Black
    Intellectual* (book by Jerry
    Gaffio Watts), 77
Hersey, John, 116
Hickman, Alonzo (character in
    Juneteenth) 3, 10, 15, 53,
    115-27, 136-38
Hicks, Granville, 70-71, 137
Hill, Patricia Liggins, 37
Hill, Robert, 46

history of rhetoric, 13, 16
Holt Street Baptist Church, 98,
    99
Howe, Irving, 2, 4, 20, 57-58,
    71-79, 139
Hubbard, Dolan, 16-17, 19, 30,
    123, 136
*Huckleberry Finn, The
    Adventures of* (novel by
    Mark Twain), 134
Hudson, Bill, 106
Hughes, Langston, 75
Hurston, Zora Neale, 76, 138

"I Have a Dream Speech," 19,
    93, 100, 101, 118
*In Search of Our Mother's
    Gardens* (essay collection
    by Alice Walker), 76

Jackson, Lawrence, 31, 58, 76,
    135
Jackson, Mahalia, 100
James, Henry, 58, 60, 70-72, 74,
    79, 81-82, 124
Jameson, Frederic, 91-94, 107,
    139
jazz, 1, 50, 59, 61, 81, 135-36
Jenkins, William A., 103
Joe Cah, 111, 123, 127-28
Johnson, Lyndon B., 2
Juneteenth (the holiday), 124

Kennedy administration, 104
Kennedy, George, 16-18
Kennedy, John F., 107, 116
Kennedy, Robert, 93
King Lear (play by William
    Shakespeare), 128·

King, Dr. Martin Luther, Jr., 3, 13, 19, 21, 29, 31-32, 52, 93, 96-107, 116-18, 124, 136, 140
Kolatch, Myron, 71-73
Kristeva, Yonka, 11

Leadbelly, 75
leadership, 8, 30-31, 40, 44-45, 47, 49, 51-52, 92-94, 101, 109
Lee, Harper, 1, 109
"Letter from a Birmingham Jail" (letter by Dr. Martin Luther King, Jr.), 103
Library of Congress, 2, 70, 79, 131
Lincoln Memorial, 100, 117-19
Lincoln, Abraham, 100, 107, 118-19, 136
Living Novel, The (collection of essays edited and compiled by Granville Hicks) 70, 137
Locke, John, 62
Lucifer, 125

Malcolm X, 21, 93, 101, 138, 140
Malraux, Andre, 75
"Man Who Lived Underground, The" (story by Richard Wright), 68
"Many Thousand Gone" (spiritual), 94, 96, 105
"Many Thousand Gone" (essay by James Baldwin), 72
March on Washington, 100, 118-19
McPherson, James Allan, 122-23, 129

McWhorter, Diane, 102-3, 105-7, 109
Melville, Herman, 59, 70, 81, 133-34, 141
Menelaus, 67-68
Miracle Sunday, 105
Moby Dick, (novel by Herman Melville), 59, 133-34
modes of production, 92
Montgomery Improvement Association, 97, 99, 117
Morrison, Toni, 50, 74, 76-77
Moton, Robert, 15
Murray, Albert, 115, 134, 138
Mysterious Stranger, The (novel by Mark Twain), 134-35
NAACP, 32, 34, 45, 97
National Book Award, 4, 60, 64, 65, 69, 79, 81, 91, 107-8, 129
Native American, 137
"negro" as a term for African Americans, 2
Negro Quarterly, 58
New Republic, 58
Nixon, E. D., 97-98
Nobel Peace Prize, 32, 107
novel form, 57-63

O'Connor, Flannery, 76
O'Meally, Robert, 82, 136
Odyssey, 67
Old Testament, 19, 100, 123, 126, 136

Paine, Albert Bigelow, 113
Parker, Charlie, 82
Parks, Rosa, 52, 97, 99

Parting the Waters (book by
    Taylor Branch), 97, 106
passion of Christ, 103
Paul of Tarsus, 36-38
peripetia, 95
Phaedrus (dialogue by Plato),
    13, 47
plasticity of the novel as a form,
    61
Plato, 13-14, 17, 47, 97, 128
political assassination, 115
political speech, 18-19, 21, 42,
    121, 136
Political Unconscious, The
    (book by Frederic Jameson),
    91, 139
Polsgrove, Carol, 77
Porter, Horace, 82
Pound, Ezra, 79
Powell, Adam Clayton, Jr., 33-
    34
Proteus, 60, 65-69

Rafferty, Terrence, 1
Ras (character in *Invisible
    Man*), 5, 7-11, 20, 28, 31,
    34, 38, 40, 44-46, 68, 93-94,
    97, 101, 104, 121, 127
realism, 62
relationship between history and
    art, 91-92, 115
rhetoric, 9, 13-19, 27, 29, 41,
    42, 44, 48, 69, 94, 97, 99,
    100-102, 104, 121-23, 127-
    29, 136, 140
"Rhetoric of Anticommunism in
    Invisible Man, The" (essay
    by Barbara Foley), 15

Rimbaud, Arthur, 1

Rinehart (character in *Invisible
    Man*), 11, 91, 102, 106,
    108-9
romance as an influence on the
    novel form, 59, 61
Rome, Italy, 115, 135
Roosevelt, Franklin, Jr., 34
Rosenwald Fellowship, 31
Rushing, Jimmy, 82
Rustin, Bayard, 100-101

Salinger, J. D., 59
Sambo the doll (figure in
    Invisible Man), 38-40
Scarlet Letter, The (novel by
    Nathaniel Hawthorne), 61
Scott, Sir Walter, 33, 61
Sekora, John, 74, 140
Senate, 3, 10, 18, 107, 111, 117,
    121-23, 127-29, 136
*Sermon and the African
    American Literary
    Imagination, The* (book by
    Dolan Hubbard), 16, 123
Severen (character in
    Juneteenth), 121, 125
Shakespeare, William, 128
Shuttlesworth, Fred, 102-4
Signifying Monkey, The (book
    by Henry Louis Gates, Jr.),
    140
Singleton, M. K., 8, 35, 45
Sister Neal (character in
    Juneteenth), 119
Socrates, 13, 14, 16, 27, 29, 30,
    42, 47, 97
Southern Christian Leadership
    Conference (SCLC), 93, 96,
    98, 102, 104

speech, 3, 4, 8-15, 18-20, 25-31,
34, 36, 38, 40-48, 50, 52,
60, 64-69, 79, 81, 91, 93,
94-102, 106, 108, 111, 117-
19, 122-23, 123-27, 136,
138
speeches, 9, 12-16, 18-19, 21,
25, 27, 40-42, 44, 50, 69,
93, 98-100
Stepto, Robert, 35, 39, 45, 51
Stowe, Harriet Beecher, 93,
107-9, 120
Student Nonviolent
Coordinating Committee
(SNCC), 93
Styron, William, 109
Sunraider, also called Bliss
(character in *Juneteenth*),
10, 18, 53, 115-37

Tarp (character in *Invisible
Man*), 35-39
Their Eyes Were Watching God
(novel by Zora Neale
Hurston), 140
theories of the novel, 60, 65
THIS IS MY BEST (literary
anthology edited by Whit
Burnett), 95
To Kill a Mockingbird (novel by
Harper Lee), 109
Tobitt (character in *Invisible
Man*), 39
Toomer, Jean, 1
Transcendentalist movement, 61
Truman, Harry S., 32, 33
Tuskegee, 15, 76
Twain, Mark, 65, 113, 134-35

Uncle Tom's Cabin (novel by
Harriet Beecher Stowe), 93,
106-7, 109, 120
United Nations, 32
Universal Negro Improvement
Association, 45, 46
Urquhart, Brian, 32

Vietnam, 2

Walker, Alice, 76
Washington, Booker T., 3, 8,
15, 26-31, 33-37, 44-45, 52,
92, 101-2, 106
Watt, Ian, 62
Watts, Jeryy Gaffio, 52, 77-78
"We Shall Overcome," 95
Westrum (character in *Invisible
Man*), 38
Word, the (as text of the Bible
or of the Constitution, used
primarily in *Juneteenth*), 53,
121, 123-26
Wright, Richard, 15, 32, 58, 68,
72-75, 77-79, 81
writer, 1, 2, 13, 15, 20, 25-26,
35-37, 39, 40, 42, 44-45,
47-48, 50-51, 53, 60, 63-65,
68, 72, 74, 75-77, 79, 81,
96, 111, 115, 133-39
writing as correlary to speech,
10-15, 20

Young, Andrew, 104

About the Author

H. William Rice is professor of English and dean of the School of Liberal Arts at Shorter College in Rome, Georgia. He has published essays on literature and the teaching of writing in a wide range of journals, including *Black American Literature Forum* (now called *African American Review*), *Education, Business Communication Quarterly*, and *CLA Journal*. He has also published articles in national magazines, such as *American Legacy*. His fiction has appeared in the *Indiana Review* and *Sporting Tales*. His first book, *Toni Morrison and the American Tradition*, was published by Peter Lang in 1996 and was reprinted in 1998. He lives in Rome, Georgia, with his wife and two sons.